CHANGING
THE SALES
CONVERSATION

CONNECT | COLLABORATE | CLOSE

LINDA RICHARDSON

New York   Chicago   San Francisco   Athens   London
Madrid   Mexico City   Milan   New Delhi
Singapore   Sydney   Toronto

1 2 3 4 5 6 7 8 9 0   QFR/QFR   1 9 8 7 6 5 4 3

ISBN   978-0-07-182365-4
MHID   0-07-182365-4

e-ISBN   978-0-07-182495-8
e-MHID   0-07-182495-2

Library of Congress Cataloging-in-Publication Data

Richardson, Linda.
   Changing the sales conversation: connect, collaborate, and close/Linda Richardson.
     pages cm
   ISBN 978-0-07-182365-4 (hardback)—ISBN0-07-182365-4 (hardback)
   1. Selling.　2. Customer relations.　I. Title.
   HF5438.25.R5126 2014
   658.85—dc23   2013033431

McGraw-Hill Education books are available at special quantity discounts to use as premiums and sales promotions or for use in corporate training programs. To contact a representative, please visit the Contact Us pages at www.mhprofessional.com.

In memory of my beloved husband Paul,
who gave so much more to my company than his name.
He inspired me to start and build Richardson and
write all of my books. He remains my strength.

Contents

Foreword

There's no better way to learn about people in depth—to get to know their every move, to understand how they think, or to predict what they will do next—than to compete against them. For many years, and with dozens of prospective clients, Linda Richardson and I were fierce competitors. Often from an initial list of eight or so contenders, she and I were almost always the last two standing. Whenever I heard that she was one of the finalists for a project where I was in the running, I knew that it would be tough; whenever she wasn't on the list I breathed a sigh of relief. We regarded each other with that unique combination of respect and visceral competitiveness that salespeople everywhere reserve for the one competitor who keeps them up at night. After a competitive sale, when I did a win–loss analysis, the feedback from clients was depressingly similar: "Linda Richardson is creative, she's smart, she knows what she's talking about, she has new ideas, she *thinks*." By definition, of course, clients are always right, so all I could do was hope that once in a while they might add, "but you do all that too, and better."

In the days when we were first going head to head against each other, there wasn't a lot of creativity or new thinking happening amongst sales training vendors. The average competitor offered the standard range of techniques that today seem so simplistic: objection handling, features and benefits, open and closed questions, and, of course, closing techniques. These ideas had been minimally repackaged from the early work of writers such as E. K. Strong in the 1920s. Fifty years later they were looking distinctly tired. Linda was one of the first people in the sales training world to realize that the old ideas were not enough. Coming from very different backgrounds, she and I were amongst the early innovators in the field who recognized that the new selling was about solutions, not about products; it was about needs, not about features.

This new thinking, variously called Consultative Selling, Solutions Selling, and Client-Centered Selling, was to change the sales world. It was a major step forward in terms of sophistication. Clients, not products, became the center of the sales effort. Opening durable, long-term relationships replaced the old focus on closing one-off deals. Understanding clients became more important than persuading them. We were enthusiastic missionaries for the new selling, and each of us was able to document some dramatic changes in sales performance in the companies that implemented our ideas. We read each other's works and learned from each other, gratefully.

Bit by bit, company by company, the new client need–based selling moved from being a revolutionary challenge to becoming the established wisdom. Nobody today would think of going back to the simplistic and manipulative techniques that dominated selling before the consultative revolution.

In a curious kind of way, history is now repeating itself. The sales revolution, which Linda played such an important role in popularizing, is itself under attack from new concepts, new technologies, and new client demands. The ideas that originally put her in the forefront of fresh thinking are themselves starting to look tired. Most people would decide that this would be a good time to bow out, having made their decisive contribution. But Linda Richardson, as her best-in-class clients will tell you, is not most people. Over the years, she has consistently renewed herself and evolved her thinking. She has remained at the *cutting edge of selling,* as her new book, *Changing the Sales Conversation,* so clearly shows. This is no mean feat. Selling is now changing more profoundly and more quickly than it has at any time in history.

There seems to be general agreement on what is driving these changes. One clear factor is the rising power of the client. Armed with sophisticated purchasing techniques and given more vendor choices than ever before, clients are not only in the driver's seat but also commandeering turbocharged juggernauts with sufficient power to crush all but the strongest and most skilled providers. The Internet has given clients omniscient access to information about their available choices. We are in a world where *how* you sell has become vastly more important that *what* you sell.

So how *do* you sell in a world where the economy has changed buyers, the client—despite having all the power—is risk averse, the competition is global, and salespeople have less leverage than ever before? Linda Richardson's answer is that salespeople, and their companies, must behave in a radically different way. The conversations they have with their clients must be very different to innovate, engage, satisfy, and keep clients. This new conversation has five distinct elements that will enable you to bring insights, ideas, and meaningful value to your clients to accelerate and close sales. You'll meet new thinking and strategies throughout the book and see how each of her five elements link into a coherent whole. It's sophisticated but actionable stuff, very different from the "magic bullet" approach of so many current sales books that offer simplistic answers to complex issues.

Like it or not, we are living in an age of complexity, and this wisdom-packed book will help you succeed in it. Linda knows what she is talking about—and listening to. These ideas and strategies are based on years of experience. Yet they are entirely new. With this book as your guide, you too can be the "last one standing" as you compete and win in an ever-shifting competitive world.

Neil Rackham
Executive Professor of Professional Selling
University of Cincinnati
Bestselling author of *SPIN Selling*

Acknowledgments

Without Them . . .

It is hard to know where to start to express my appreciation for not only the number of supporters that have made this book possible but also the level of support they have given to me. I feel so lucky to have had the rare opportunity to pioneer Consultative Selling, to have played a part in the move to online learning, and now to contribute to the new sales conversation.

My gratitude goes to the smart and demanding clients, the sales leaders, salespeople, and human resource professionals who have honored me with their trust through the years. My deepest appreciation goes to my once tough competitor and now colleague and good friend Neil Rackham who has been so very generous with his time and insights and who has enriched my ideas and encouraged my voice in these pages. Thanks goes to my friend and colleague Jonathan Farrington who has opened the door to global collaboration, which has been important to me. I thank Ian MacMillian, my department head at Wharton, for his early and lasting support and guidance. I thank Alex Lajoux who inspires me with her creative thinking and effervescent spirit and Rose Biscotti Stowell, my friend and valued colleague. My thanks also goes to Donya Dickerson, my longtime editor who has championed my books and exemplifies publishing excellence.

After so many years as their colleague, I thank the Richardson teams past and present, and in particular all the designers and administrative assistants who too often are the unsung heroes but who make a difference in the lives of so many professionals.

The book of selling will never come to an end. To offer new chapters is an honor—one that belongs not only to me but also to the many who have been my guides.

1

Introduction

"Your sales conversation is the most important sales tool you have."

"What's changed? Everything."

In this era of iPads, iPhones, and apps, sales communications may be growing, but sales conversations are dying—and so are many sales. This book, the product of several decades developing hundreds of thousands of salespeople all over the world, is not about how to sell but about how to sell *differently*. It guides you in how to use the new links and technologies without losing sight of the very reason for making a connection in the first place—a chance to exchange ideas in conversations that lead to winning business and long-term relationships.

When I first began working with sales forces to improve their sales performance, sales talk had historically been a monologue. Salespeople talked. Clients listened. Salespeople had to know about their products but not much about their clients. This approach worked well enough for that era because clients had fewer options and no way to learn about their products other than through salespeople.

But as things progressed and competition started to heat up it was clear to me that salespeople had to become more client focused and solutions more customized. I knew the power of dialogue from my background in psychology and education. I was instrumental in establishing selling as a two-way conversation based on needs and customized solutions. Back then I talked with sales leaders about strategy and process and provided salespeople with skills and techniques to help them be more successful. The hot topic was creating a dialogue to *uncover* client needs and customize solutions. For most organizations, the transition to the need dialogue was not easy. Salespeople had to unlearn decades of making "one-size-fits-all," standardized, and script-like product pitches and learn how to ask questions and tailor solutions to client needs.

I taught consultative skills and techniques *because they worked* and were instrumental in helping salespeople make the shift needed to succeed. The sales environment of the times supported this approach.

Clients were more patient—actually, appreciative—and would educate salespeople. Clients shared their needs, giving salespeople the information and time required to shape customized solutions.

Now something new has happened. You are aware there is a new sales landscape—one that is more complex and challenging than ever before. You know your clients are smarter and scoping out their own needs and solutions before they contact you. Yet, if you ask most salespeople today what their job is, they tell you something to the effect of convincing clients that their offerings are superior to their competition's. Just a very short time ago that would have been a reasonable answer. But clients today have what seems like limitless quality choices, and product superiority is harder to prove. It is not what you know about your products that clients value, but what you can do with what you know to solve their business problems. Clients must believe you *understand* their business challenges and that you are prepared to drive results. They expect you to anticipate their needs and add to what they know. They look for insights, ideas, and know-how. For most salespeople shifting their conversations from product to business challenges is a leap, not a tweak. For decades there has been no fundamental changes to selling and no impetus to radically change selling models—but that is no longer the case.

Today both you and your clients have other ways of finding information about each other and no longer depend solely on dialogue. Every day you start your day getting ready for your calls, anxious about the pressure but driven to achieve. With one click on a website you can enter your client's world. Your clients are doing just that to learn about your and your competitors' offerings. Information is everywhere and everyone is tapping into it.

> "Chance favors the connected mind."
> —Steven Johnson, author of Where Good Ideas Come From

In the new sales environment the tough news is that you will fail if you do only the things that made you successful just a few short years ago. Some of those things will actually hurt you. The changes in how clients buy are profound. Today, sales strategy, process, skills, and tools are the province of anyone who wants to be successful. The boundaries between what sales managers and salespeople must know have blurred. The boundaries between selling and marketing have blurred. And most significantly the boundaries and expectations between you and your clients have blurred.

> *"There is an absence of new sales models and many of the old ones are not working."*
> —Neil Rackham

Clients were the experts in their business and you in yours. Today clients and their teams are searching the Web, spending hours at whiteboards figuring out their needs, studying their alternatives, and encroaching on the product knowledge/solution terrain that once belonged to you. Clients turn to the Internet and no longer solely rely on sales conversations to learn about the options available to them. They are not interested in hearing a delineation of your product capabilities. Differentiation is not in your products. It is your expertise. You have become the differentiator.

There is an immediate need for most salespeople to change their sales conversations. In this book we will focus on five strategies needed to move your conversations from product to business outcomes to succeed in the new sales landscape:

Futuring: Meta-Preparation

Call it prognostication. Call it clairvoyance. Today you have to be one step ahead of your clients. Every salesperson has some vision of the future. But in the past selling worked according to a different time horizon. Today's clients are looking to you for insights and ideas to expand beyond what they already know to help them solve not just their current but also their emerging business challenges.

Heat-Mapping: Anticipating Client Needs

Your clients have done their homework. They've researched their issues, compared their solution options, and come to the sales table smarter. The days of their answering a long list of discovery questions are gone. Diagnosing needs is no longer the conversation starter. Your role is to turn up the heat by raising the visibility of priority business challenges and demonstrating that you understand their world. From your first client conversation clients expect you to show that you can add value. You too must be smarter and engage them with questions that move from discovery to collaboration. The new need conversation is one in which you teach and learn.

Value-Tracking: Shaping Solutions

Just a short time ago clients defined value in terms of the quality of the performance of products. They compared how well competitors' products satisfied their needs. Today value is defined in terms of outcomes and financial impact. Differentiation is what *you* bring to the table. The bar has been raised on the expertise you must have to sell and on the breath and scope of what it takes to configure a winning solution.

Phasing: Controlling the Process

Your clients' buying cycle has changed. Clients now control the sales process. From their perspective buying has become a problem-solving cycle. When you enter their buying cycle determines in large part how much influence you have and your success in closing. A defined sales process gives you a strong competitive advantage. It is key to moving deals through the pipeline quickly and to forecasting accurately.

Linking: Connecting Emotionally

Linking is more than ice breaking. Linking is the thorniest of all of the strategies ; it is not only the one everyone takes for granted but it also connects all of the above. In a world where it is easy to think technology and information rule, your clients are still looking for something you won't find in their requests for proposals. Certainly they demand expertise and metrics, but the role emotions play in their decision making cannot be underestimated. Yes, you must connect the dots, but you must also connect person to person. It is the art of being both client-centered and human-centered.

The five strategies in this book are about adapting quickly to the sweeping changes in today's selling landscape. This book has one overriding goal: to provide you with the know-how to solve your clients' business challenges and help you reach your goals on the new sales map.

Fundamental Shifts

Globalization, the economy, and emerging technologies have unhinged selling and profoundly changed how clients buy. These factors have converged to create the new sales landscape:

Globalization

With more than 200 sovereign nations in the world, each with some ability to market something virtually, globalization, conservatively speaking, has doubled the number of competitors. Client choices have

exploded geometrically, making it more difficult for you to differentiate on product, quality, or price. Addi-
tionally, competitors can come from
anywhere in the world. In the past,
what law firm could have imagined,
for example, that it would be competing for business and would lose
40 percent of its legal research billing
to a competitor in another country?

> *". . . and a dialogue leads to connection which leads to trust which leads to engagement."*
> —Seth Godin

The Path of Knowledge

The real significance to you of the explosion in competition goes
beyond navigating a tougher and more crowded competitive landscape. It has made the old model of selling, which relied on selling
the better mousetrap, irrelevant. Clients believe any number of
providers can meet their needs equally well. Differentiation, not
product quality, is the pressure point.

In the old days the sales message, for customized and non-
customized solutions, was, "Let me tell you about my product and
why it is better." Clients have other resources and no longer depend
on you to learn about products. Moreover, a major study by the Corporate Executive Board (CEB) tells us that clients are 57 percent
through their buying cycle before talking to a salesperson. Clients are
conducting their own research and then turning to their peers and
social networking for unbiased information before turning to you.

But what does this really tell you? For starters, clients are more
informed and there is the danger of their treating your solution as
a commodity. But it does not tell you that clients no longer need
you. Access to knowledge goes both ways, and you can be just as
informed as your clients and more so. Even though clients have
unprecedented access to knowledge, they face the difficulty of

sorting through what matters most and finding the value among all the options. Knowledge and *know-how* are two different things. That is where you come in. Even with clients who are deeper into their buying cycle, you can bring expertise, relevant insights, and ideas that reshape their thinking and influence their buying decisions in your favor.

> *"Ch ch ch changes . . ."*
> —David Bowie

The best salespeople have always brought ideas and created value for their clients. But now the ability to deliver superior value cannot be limited to a select few. It has become a requirement for any salesperson who wants to succeed in sales.

Risk Aversion

It is no surprise to you that the economy has changed how, why, and when your clients buy. Because of the uncertainty of the economy clients are highly risk averse. Decisions are being made by consensus. To avoid mistakes clients are tapping into trusted colleagues, consultants, and advisors to narrow down the providers *they* will contact. They are demanding proof of value not in terms of product superiority but financial impact. Spending is under a microscope and solutions must not only satisfy the client's direct needs but also meet cross-functional objectives and support corporate goals.

Kicked Upstairs

The concern about risk has in turn elevated the buying decision to the executive suite. Decisions formerly made by midlevel managers are now in the C-suite where the language of risk and value, not features and benefits, is spoken. Executives are getting involved in deals far smaller than ever before, and you face the challenge of engaging them at a strategic level. Clients are demanding more consulting and support but at the same time demanding pricing more appropriate to transactional sales where no or little innovation, advice, or implementation support is needed.

Technology

The Internet and emerging technologies have had a profound impact on how clients buy. Your clients have embraced technology. The convergence of technologies has created the single most transformational change in the history of selling. It has altered how information is exchanged, making it possible for people to talk to each other at any time in multiple formats and get almost any information they want in real time. It has disseminated knowledge, making clients smarter and more independent. It has raised their expectations. It has redefined how they buy, how they acquire knowledge, and what they value from you. It has created a knowledge explosion that has turned knowledge into a commodity and put a premium on your ability to bring clients relevant insight, ideas, and solutions.

Many clients may be ahead of you in maximizing technology, and they are getting better and better at buying. If they have surpassed you, you must vigorously embrace technology and choose the key sales tools needed to respond, build your knowledge portfolio, and maximize your time.

Conversations to Teach and Learn

With such dramatic changes in how clients buy, it would seem reasonable to tell you that there is an entirely new way to sell and it is time to leave everything you know about selling behind. But that's absolutely not so. *Yes, selling as we knew it is gone, and the parts that have changed are so significant that if you don't master them you will struggle to be relevant to your clients.* There is no question—you must sell differently. At the same time though, *you must not lose the consultative skills* that helped you communicate and build relationships with your clients. Your consultative selling skills are still relevant—they are the platform for reaching the next level.

> *"The impact of technology is exponential . . . We won't experience 100 years of progress in the 21st century—it will be more like 20,000 years of progress."*
> —Kurt Kurzweil, Director of Engineering, Google

Clients have evolved so quickly. There is an urgency for you to change many of the sales models that have been baked into your sales approach. A recent research study by Forrester reported that a scant 15 percent of senior decision makers interviewed felt their meetings with salespeople were *valuable.* This is a serious incitement.

What clients were looking for and not getting is business acumen and deeper expertise to solve their current and future business challenges. Today's clients expect dialogues brimming with subject matter expertise—but the subject has changed. Expertise on your product capabilities is the price of admission, and so are your skills. The expertise that matters is around insights and ideas and what you know about your client's industries, their companies, and them. Teaching now holds a high place in your portfolio of skills. But the teaching must be collaborative, positioning you as teacher and learner.

Based on my extensive experience in working with hundreds of thousands of salespeople, salespeople who serve up insights and ideas have always existed—but they have always been in the minority. These top performers consistently have made up about 10 percent of a sales force. This elite group are the the legends and luminaries who bring value to clients far beyond their product capabilities in the form of advice and problem solving. No longer can that kind of performance be the province of only the legends and luminaries. In the new sales environment, there is little room for the average performers that sustained sales organizations for decades. Google's mantra that "great is not good enough" is the message of sales today. You must demonstrate greater expertise, stronger skills, more creativity, and deeper motivation. *The new sales conversation is no longer a Q&A between buyer and seller. It is a conversation between business equals in productive collaboration.*

Your sales conversation is still your most important sales tool. Technology is the vehicle. Knowledge is the content. Clients' voices are loud. Context and content are king. But you are the connector.

Perhaps your sales organization is grappling to find answers and make the changes needed in its selling system. Ideally it is supporting you with knowledge sharing, messaging, and sales tools. Firms such as Aberdeen Group, Bersin Deloitte, CSO Insights, ES Research Group, Forrester, Sales Executive Council, Richardson, and ZS Research document what best-in-class organizations and salespeople are doing. Everyone in sales is bombarded with unprecedented mounds of data about client behavior, buying practices, and best practices in selling—much of which is insightful and helpful, some of which is contradicting. But all of the data shows there is no turning back the clock. The paths of knowledge will continue to change, but your role as a salesperson will be even more important as you bring relevant expertise, insights, and ideas to your clients.

Change and Challenge

This is a time of great opportunity. In a sense, all sales organizations and salespeople are in "start-up" mode on an equal footing in this new world. There are many salespeople who are clinging to their glory days and the ways that worked for them in the past. Others are experimenting with different ways of relating to clients. Undoubtedly, if you are successful, you are already using many of the new ideas and skills I present in this book. You may be using them without ascribing a name to them. This book will help you understand and master the five strategies that will enable you to engage in meaningful conversations your clients value and for which you are well rewarded.

Today's economy is facilitated by technology. The technology available to you is game changing. But this book is about *you* and your expertise, passion, and commitment to build relationships in the true sense of the word *relationship*—a series of sales based on the value you bring and the trust you earn. This book is about adapting to the present and looking into the future. It is about understanding the changes happening in sales and acting differently because of them. It is about connecting on a business and personal level, collaborating as an equal, and closing more business every day. It will help you tweak what needs tweaking and change what needs changing to succeed in your sales role as an advisor your clients trust—a problem solver, teacher, and learner.

> *"The definition of insanity is doing the same thing and expecting different results."*
> *—Albert Einstein*

Your smarter clients are already out there—savvy, busy, pressured, risk averse, and in need of guidance to make the best business and personal decisions. Transformation comes from change, not the other way around. Your clients have already changed. Buyers' habits are changing fast. You too have been making adjustments. The sales conversation and scorecard are new. Now it's time to *challenge yourself to change*—for your clients, your sales organization, and yourself. There is a new breed of buyers and sellers. It is now time to start to change your sales conversation. Let's begin together.

2

Futuring: Meta-Preparation

"Sales has become more of a conversation between business equals, not a seller pitching a buyer."

There is a radically new order to selling. The huge migration to the Internet and mobile devices has changed what your clients know and how and where they buy. They have fingertip access to a massive amount of knowledge, which has made them smarter. They come to the sale meta-prepared. *Meta* is the Greek word for beyond, and that is what is required of your preparation because clients expect you to know about their industry, business, and them *before* you meet with them. They expect you to *add* to what they already know.

While your clients are working to find ideas and solutions among the flood of information on their screens every day, you too must be building your knowledge, skills, and experience so you can meet their expectations with insights, informed questions, and fresh ideas that help them grow their businesses. Being able to differentiate yourself in this new world demands an unprecedented level of preparation.

A few years ago an experienced salesperson who conducted a solid review of a client's website, annual report, and relationship file was ready for most client meetings. This is not to say in any way that selling was easy or that preparation wasn't important. But clients weren't self-educating at the pace and level they are today. They have taken the reigns of the sale. But you can regain control and share those reigns with "touch" research through several searches and using the powerful sales tools available to you. Clients are using social media tools and other platforms to access and share information, and if you want to know what's on their minds you must use the same tools and platforms and more.

> *"Smart is about information. Once you have information and understand it and know what to do with it, you are halfway to smart."*
> —Guru Banovar, Chief Technology Officer, IBM

Your challenge is to learn faster than your clients and your competitors. Winning requires an urgency to learn new things, create value, and earn trust.

Meta-Preparation

Fortunately, in the digital age deeper and broader preparation is faster and easier than ever before, enabling you to add value from the first conversation. Building your expertise is as much a mindset as a strategy. It's having zero tolerance for wasting time—your client's or yours. It takes curiosity. It takes creativity. It takes discipline and focus. Meta-preparation enables you to understand not only the industry, the inner workings of the department you are selling to, and the preferences of the key stakeholders but also the groups within the organization that will be affected by your solutions. In simple terms it is understanding that "the hip bone is connected to the thigh bone" so you can gain consensus and configure complex and/or cross-functional solutions.

You likely have a depth of knowledge about the products in your portfolio. Forrester reported that 88 percent of the executives in its Executive Insight Survey felt that salespeople were knowledgeable about their products, while 55 percent thought that

> *Basic data is a commodity thanks to Internet free availability."*
> *—Aberdeen Group*

salespeople were knowledgeable about their clients' industries (which is only about half of the salespeople selling to them). Worse yet, only a startling 6 percent of executives felt that the agenda of salespeople was to help them drive results. And it is worth repeating that Forrester tells us that only 15 percent of executive buyers find their meetings with salespeople valuable.

Your knowledge of your products has meaning to clients only when it relates to helping them drive results. Clearly, conversations must change, and to make the change deeper, industry, company, and stakeholder knowledge is demanded.

In the recent past it was not only acceptable but also expected that you would ask clients to tell you about their business and that you would educate them on your capabilities. Today clients will respond to that level of straight discovery question and product talk with impatience. Conversations easily will be cut short. Clients want to be educated but not about products. They want new perspectives and ideas that produce outcomes. You must be ahead of them, and if your knowledge is steps behind, selling will be an uphill battle.

Be Performance Ready

The two critical areas of knowledge for you to focus on are:

- Industry knowledge that gives you a running start in understanding your markets and businesses and makes conversations, even with new clients, feel like familiar territory

- Company and stakeholder knowledge that allows you to anticipate and meet your clients' current and emerging needs

Be Industry Ready

You already know that the world of selling has become more connected and specialized. When you are industry ready you understand your clients' worlds and you keep up to date with the rapid changes. Industry knowledge is an essential part of business acumen. For example, if you are selling to DHL, you are expected to know the transportation and logistics space.

To understand an industry look at both the external forces that affect it, such as regulations, and the internal challenges and opportunities it faces, such as management issues. Many problem points are common across companies in a given industry and across industries, and you can leverage these points. For example, if you are selling technology solutions to digital marketing companies, you

> *"'Marketing needs to get a deep understanding of customers' business needs in order to prep sales reps appropriately."*
> *—Fabio Paiano, IMAGAEM*

should know the impact of October 2013 privacy regulations on solicitation and the meteoric rise in litigation. While industry knowledge is not specific to any particular company, it speeds up client preparation, provides language to draw on to explore business challenges, spurs insights and ideas, and increases your confidence in making recommendations.

Depending on how your organization is structured, you may or may not be expected to serve as the formal subject matter expert (SME). Nonetheless, even if there are designated SMEs you must be able to connect your product, industry, and client knowledge with the business outcomes that are important to your clients. For example, when a generalist salesperson who sold novelty gifts read in her local paper that 70 percent of the clients of a national sports chain were women but only 10 percent of the chain's products were geared toward women, she made a connection between the business gap and an idea she could bring to the client. Understanding that retail was suffering and that sales in sporting goods stores were down significantly, especially among chains, she sent a *letter* to the chain's president. She shared an insight along with a high-level overview of her idea to expand its offerings to women and supported that with revenue projections. She followed up with an e-mail invitation. Within a week she met with the president, the executive vice president (EVP) of purchasing, and a marketing officer. Three months later she signed a large contract (using electronic signature) with the parent company. Not to let a good idea and success story go to waste, she transplanted that solution and won business with another sporting goods chain.

> *"The greatest danger in times of turbulence is not the turbulence; it is to respond with yesterday's logic."*
> —Peter Drucker

With a deep understanding of your industry segments and verticals you can demonstrate to your clients that you can create value. You can anticipate their needs, develop insights, and create sales opportunities rather than wait for requests for proposals. Whether you use client analytics that your company provides for you or participate in industry trade shows where you meet clients, see what they are interested in, and experience competitors' offerings, it is crucial that you become industry smart. And with each new bit of industry knowledge that you gain, ask yourself, "How can I apply this to my clients? With whom can I share this? How shall I share it?"

Technology has made selling smarter easier, but this new sales environment demands working harder. You are probably already working longer hours, using search engines to visit industry sites, delving into current research, and joining relevant industry groups in Google and LinkedIn—if not, do so ASAP. But you must do more.

Tap into all the resources available to you:

- Read industry white papers issued by firms that focus on verticals.
- Ask clients about the industry and social media groups they belong to and join them.
- Visit industry association websites, sign up for their mailings, and read their blogs.

■ Use alerts offered by industry publications.

■ Follow trade associations' sites to identify trends and issues.

■ Read what your clients read such as industry journals or blogs.

■ Follow business analysts' reports that cover your clients' industries to identify trends and forces affecting them, such as the economy, markets, or legislation.

■ Identify the top industry publication, read it, and share with your clients articles that might interest them.

■ Actively use social media to find a need or niche in which you can add value and specialize.

■ Participate in industry conversations and engage with peers to understand the hot issues.

■ Take online university courses, many of which are offered noncredited for free at universities such as Wharton, Stanford, Harvard, and MIT.

■ Join industry groups and business associations to broaden your knowledge and contacts.

■ Buy a share of your public clients' stock to get up-to-the-minute information and analysts' perspectives.

■ Learn from clients and colleagues, and play it forward.

■ Participate in industry trade shows and conferences.

Being industry ready sets the foundation, but industry knowledge is "one to all." As important as it is, it doesn't replace doing homework on your clients' companies and their stakeholders. You are not selling to customer groups. You are selling to individual buyers.

Be Company and Stakeholder Ready

In the Forrester Insight Survey only 38 percent of executives felt that salespeople understood the issues facing the executives and only 34 percent felt that salespeople were able to relate to the executives' roles. You are already learning about your clients from their websites, LinkedIn, and Facebook when you gather business and personal insights and reach and connect with them. The problem is that your competitors are doing the same thing. As informative as these resources are, the question is how can you learn even more about your clients. To anticipate clients' needs and solve their business challenges you must determine what is on their mind and their agenda—and what they are missing.

As you analyze a company to identify its goals, objectives, challenging issues, and strategic initiatives to identify potential issues and opportunities, research all of the stakeholders. Start by identifying their functional roles and responsibilities and work to learn about their role in the decision-making process, political alignment, buying behavior, desired outcomes, and personal needs.

Analyze the company and stakeholders:

■ Start by reviewing *every page* on a client's website to understand their vision, products, and goals for being in the marketplace. Go to the career tab to understand the qualities, competencies, and values the company looks for in the people it hires and likely seeks in its salespeople. Websites give you a view of how clients see themselves and how they want to be perceived. Make a list of what you find relevant on the website to reference when you speak with them. For example, if a company underscores its innovation, compliment and probe that. Work in what is cutting edge about your company as it relates to the client's current and future goals. While the website is an important source of client knowledge, it is merely the face the company is putting forward.

Dig deeper to understand the needs the client is focused on and even deeper to anticipate needs that you can surface.

■ Set Internet alerts such as Google Alerts or InsideView for the companies you follow by client name and division, product, and geography to keep informed about the latest changes. To help you gain insights, set alerts for your competitors, your clients' competitors, and your own company as well, which are sources many salespeople miss.

■ Look up classification codes to determine where the companies you are pursuing stand. Use this information to help you prioritize opportunities and identify business challenges your clients are facing.

■ Research your clients' competitors to understand what they are doing and to help your clients respond.

■ Research your client's customers.

■ Use social media to gather intelligence and use advanced search.

■ Find out how your clients use social media. Be socially connected and be where your clients are to learn what interests them and what they are thinking. Actively follow them on sites such as LinkedIn, Facebook, and Twitter, and read their blogs. Share your expertise to make it easy for them to find you. Learn how your clients use social media, and visit the sites that influence them. Follow whom they follow. For example, Marc won a $2.2 million, four-year contract in part by positioning his solution point by point to match the corporate values the CEO espoused in his blog.

■ Meet with your clients' marketing team to learn what *their* clients are thinking and to review the feedback their clients are giving them.

- Listen to industry analyses, read reports and press releases, and conduct name searches on the websites for the *Wall Street Journal* and the *New York Times*.

Recent research on the massive appeal of social media sheds a light on clients' stampede to social networks. A large study by Euro Economics at Claremont University on the effect of social networks on stress confirmed that brains are social animals and that visiting sites such as LinkedIn and industry sites are viewed as social interactions, naturally producing high levels of oxytocin among users and leading to increased levels of happiness and decreased levels of stress.

It is important to show you are a part of your clients' network. Join where they are and where they enjoy getting and giving influential information. Social media has created a dialogue to be read. It presents an opportunity to find out what clients are and are not looking at, which can help you understand the challenges that are high on their priority list and the ones that you can amplify. Become a part of the circle they like and trust.

Ron, a top performer, says he lives by social media and sales tools such as Google Alerts to keep abreast of management changes, new contacts, product launches, shifts in strategy, and pertinent news articles related to the companies in his territory. This early knowledge allows him to proactively approach his clients. When he learned through Jigsaw that one of his prospects had raised 50 million dollars for international expansion, he sent an e-mail in which he identified his company's access to a network of worldwide developers. He leveraged elements of a solution his team developed for another client, and based on his knowledge sharing he secured a meeting. The client said, "As you can imagine I got a lot of calls after our deal was made public, but your e-mail got my attention because it was relevant and not annoying." Ron shared an insight that led to a sale.

As you conduct your research you might be surprised how much you can learn about even your most important clients, who you thought you knew well. The expertise you build will reflect in every aspect of your sales conversation whether you are credentialing yourself in your introduction, resolving objections, asking insightful and informed questions, sharing ideas, or closing.

As you do your research, you likely are already analyzing your competitors' strengths and weaknesses and making comparisons to your offerings. But you can gain even more leverage by understanding your clients' competitors and what they are doing to stay ahead. Bringing that kind of insight to your clients is invaluable to them and allows you to create awareness of the issues your clients should be focusing on and how you can help them excel.

Building deep industry, company, and stakeholder knowledge is essential to developing insights. It is the path to differentiation and success.

Insight Readiness
Understanding Insights

Insight has become a catchword in sales. *Client insight* is a marketing term that refers to the data that is gathered about clients to predict their future needs and shape their current ones. In a marketing sense the predictions refer to a generalized population of clients, not to individual clients. Your job is to ensure the insights you bring to your clients are relevant and specific to them.

What exactly is an insight? An insight is literally a *sight from within* in that it provides a deeper understanding of what you know and *what you think* about what you know. It is a new thought, perspective, or way to solve or look at a new or existing problem. When you share insights with clients you cause them to reconsider their current thinking or practices and challenge the status quo.

Marketing guru Jeremy Bullmore defined insights with a question: "Why is insight like a refrigerator? Because the moment you look into it a light comes on." When you share an insight, to get your clients to "look into the refrigerator" and become illuminated. That insight must be relevant and presented in a way that stimulates discussion. An insight isn't an insight until the light goes on for the client. The only way to know if that has happened is to ask for the client's perceptions or experience. Insights challenge the status quo persuasively when you explore them together with your client.

Insights are knowledge at work. They connect two points and as a result trigger new thinking. But while knowledge is a factor in arriving at insights, there is also a strong element of intuition and mystery in the leap from knowledge to insight. Insights, knowledge, and ideas are connected, but they are not one and the same.

Knowledge is what you know. Knowledge is easily accessible online. Insights are not. Knowledge has long been equated with power but today has become commoditized. Nevertheless, knowledge, whether from experience, research, or intuition, helps spark insights.

Insights are not the same as ideas, but they do lead to ideas. In fact, one insight can spawn many ideas. For example, an insight might be that fluctuations in production due to inclement weather add 12 percent to production costs and create client dissatisfaction. Ideas to solve the problem could be to build storage capabilities on site to avoid the fluctuations and maintain client satisfaction or to partner with local distributors. Ideas, not insights, are actionable.

Insights are powerful because they:

- Raise the heat on an issue by challenging the status quo.

- Create urgency to change the status quo.

- Provide a perspective the client has not considered.

- Open up strategic business conversations.

- Pave the way for you to access seniors.

- Build your credibility and position yourself as a thought partner.

- Create a compelling reason to change the status quo immediately.

Some of the insights you share will add a new perspective to the way your clients think about a priority that is already on their agenda. Other insights will raise clients' awareness of a problem or opportunity that you feel should be on their agenda. An insight does not have to be major. It could be a small tweak that makes a big difference. There is probably nothing that will impress, and possibly unnerve, clients more than your making them aware of risks, potential threats, or blind spots they have missed or undervalued. By being industry and client ready, leveraging your exposure to multiple organizations, and maximizing your team and resources you are in an excellent position to bring insights to your clients that they otherwise would not see.

Developing Insights

Unless you can draw from the highest level of situational knowledge, it is unlikely that you can produce relevant insights on the spot. The open question is, how can you develop insights that are meaningful to your clients? In truth, as a salesperson or sales leader you can only be expected to do so much. While there are resources that you can tap into, corporate should in large part bear the responsibility of developing insights—whether through sales, marketing, sales operations, or an outside resource—and these should be provided to salespeople to personalize for their clients.

Ideally your marketing and sales operations groups are providing support with research and tools. According to a recent report from the Aberdeen Group, companies that use predictive client analytics on how and why clients buy achieved a 73 percent higher lift in sales than companies that do not use tools to get a full view of their clients. No one would disagree that listening to clients and acting on the insights gained are important, yet research shows that only about 25 percent of companies are giving their salespeople this competitive edge. In my experience many of the best-in-class marketing departments distribute content marketing to clients to get their attention and drive action. The question is, how many of those marketing departments are distributing insights to their sales forces?

A marketing group in a best-in-class technology company provides its salespeople with Message Maps. These Message Maps give salespeople core value messages, actionable intelligence, and insights they customize to bring value to their clients. While up to 70 percent of marketing material is not useful to or used by salespeople, the company's Message Maps are embraced by almost the entire sales force. Another company known for its excellent research reports, which are usually five or six pages in length, provides its salespeople with CliffsNotes-style briefs that salespeople use to enrich their client conversations. With or without organizational support there is absolutely no escaping the need for you to build your expertise to bring insights and ideas to your clients. Fortunately, tools and resources exist and are available to you. (Please see enablement tools later in Chapter 2.)

The Well of Insights

There are multiple sources to tap in order to develop insights. One of the best sources is your own company. It is chock-full of insights. Your company may well have solved a version of the problem your client is facing. In most sales organizations the challenge is to access the examples, best practices, and success stories. To develop insights and ideas turn to areas in your organization such as marketing, sales operations, finance, product management, and client service. Find ways to support your team members, build relationships with them, and understand what they do and what problems they have solved for their clients. *Find out what they need from you.* Research by Chally showed that the key consistent differentiator between the top 20 percent of sales performers and their counterparts is that the top 20 percent "manipulate" their own organizations—so much so that they consume the highest percentage of their companies' resources. How much of your company's resources are you leveraging?

Develop insights by leading client strategy meetings with your team members. Share your analysis of a client's business challenge, experience, and knowledge, and agree on a plan of action. You will not only be smarter for your clients but you will strengthen your internal relationships and foster team ownership as well.

Data and research are other important sources for developing insights and providing validation for your point of view. For example, Jon used research to raise his client's awareness of an alternative that would provide significant cost savings:

> We are seeing that controlling defaults has become a big issue in the industry (positioned the challenge). Technology advancements have enabled . . . Defaults have risen in . . . by 18 percent in the past 6 months. One of our large banking clients reduced default calculation times from 96 hours to just four hours and realized a savings of . . . (supported with research and return on investment [ROI]). Based on . . . I was thinking about your . . . and the potential for you to reduce . . . (showed relevance to client). Traditionally defaults are

handled ... but with ... I know how important ... is at this time and that there is a way to ... (made comparison). What has been your experience with defaults (probed client perception)?

But developing insights takes more than research and data. Rachel Schutt, a senior statistician at Google Research, at the MIT Conference in December 2012 described what makes a good data scientist: "You also want someone who has a deep, wide-ranging *curiosity*, is *innovative*, and is *guided by experience as well as data*." Developing insights requires that you are curious, critical, and skeptical in questioning the status quo and challenging your own assumptions.

Social media is another source of insights. For example, Bill landed a meeting with a chief marketing officer based on information he found on an industry blog and a comment he read on the company's Twitter feed about how the CEO was championing a voice of the customer (VOC) initiative. He created an opportunity by sharing an insight:

I understand the kind of effort that goes into a VOC initiative with analyzing valuable customer feedback and the cost of gaining that feedback (positioned the challenge). In the recent ... CRM study published in ... the two major obstacles identified in voice of customer initiatives were getting to the right customers and generating customer action ... In the study only 42 percent ... but when ... increased to 73 percent ... (supported with research and ROI). With your ... we see the opportunity to (showed relevance to client) ... rather than .... (made comparison) What has been your experience has been with your VOC initiative so far (probed client perception)?

Clients are another important source of insights. Observe them. Check out their websites' investor page and president's message. Look at them with a fresh set of eyes and question what they are doing and why they are doing it. Take the time to prepare informed questions to identify how, on what, and where they spend their time, what compelling event is forcing them to take an action, what their short- and long-term initiatives are, and what challenges are on the front and back burners. Strategize how to get to seniors. Identify the key issues that they are grappling with. For example, Tracy won a large mobile phone contract because she alone among seven competitors got to the CFO to identify and address his concerns about the lack of transparency in billing, the confusing billing statements, and billing averages.

In phrasing insights avoid all broad, sweeping statements or exaggerated language such as *all of the experts, all of our clients, all of your competitors,* or *we guarantee* when you share an insight. Clients are consuming content in very thin slices. What you say must be accurate, supported with data, and used to open up an informed dialogue.

As you develop insights leverage:

- Research

- Relevant views of thought leaders in and outside your firm

- Knowledge you gather from collaboration with your team and other departments

- Your experience

- Your observations and what you think about them

- Practices of your client's competitors and organizations they admire

- What you have gleaned from other parts of the client's organization

Creating Your Brand

The first impression you make with a prospect can be by phone, online, in person, or your profile on LinkedIn. You are living in the digital era, and that means curating your online identity and establishing your brand. How are you putting your voice in the social world? Do your clients see you as a contributor? When they look for content, do they find you?

To establish your industry presence:

- Create a credible and strong profile on sites such as LinkedIn and Facebook. Your clients will likely check you out on LinkedIn. Update it regularly. Include a picture that represents how you want your clients to think of you—what image do you want to present? Consider changing your bio so that who you are as a person is not hidden behind your credentials. Include what your clients get as a result of all your experience, expertise, and credentials. Add a human element.

- Participate in community or industry conversations, ideally weekly. Share your expertise and post ideas and approaches to address issues.

- Post questions to create a presence and start a dialogue.

- Create a blog and tweet if you enjoy writing and have something to say (if your company's policy permits blogging and tweeting).

- At a minimum read and respond to relevant blogs to stay current.

- Develop a niche so that your clients view you as the "go-to person," whether it is for industry knowledge, finance, technical strength, creativity, or getting things done.

- Join and participate in relevant client and industry groups.

- Create a short video.

- Maximize sales and social media sites such as Sales Playbook, Sales 2.0, and Sales and Marketing; sales resources sites including SalesPro, CustomerThink, Top Sales World, *Selling Power*, Richardson, CSO Insights, Corporate Executive Board, SalesBenchmark Index; and blogs and articles by experts including Dr. Tony Alessandra, Skip Anderson, Joanne Black, Jeff Blount, Dave Brock, Jonathan Farrington, Jeffrey Gitomer, Geoffrey James, Gerhard Gschwandtner, Anthony Iannarino, Dave Kurlan, Jill Konrath, Paul McCord, Nancy Nardin, Lori Richardson, Tamata Schenk, and Dave Stein. The list of talent available to you, often without charge, is extensive.

These are just a few of the thought-provoking and educational resources available to help you learn and create your online presence.

Be prepared to credentialize yourself with your clients to establish your professional and personal credibility. Typically you credential yourself at the beginning of the call during the opening. An effective opening follows a pattern like this: introduction, rapport, recap of last contact, leveraging of your preparation, credentialing, and bridge to the new need dialogue. In the new sales conversation credentialing takes on even greater significance because clients are sizing up the expertise they can expect from you. To credentialize yourself, be brief and prepared—start with relevant historical background, move to your current role and the value/expertise you are prepared to bring, and be prepared to end on a personal note that is appropriate and relevant to the client.

Sales-Ready Tool

Your clients' business challenges are increasingly complex, and the conversation you lead must address that complexity in a way that is compelling and complete but easy for your clients to follow. Using a planning tool, ideally integrated into your CRM, will help you prepare and execute an effective conversation whether face to face, on the phone (and up to 50 percent of high-end sales activity is by phone), via video conference, etc. (Please see Appendix for model planning tool.)

> *"The right sales tools will change your life."*
> —Nancy Nardin,
> Smart Selling Tools

Embrace Technology

Technology has revolutionized selling. The right sales-enablement tools dramatically improve sales performance. They make you smarter and help you get a view into your client's future. They equip you with knowledge and help you develop insights. Tools help you access markets and clients. Brainshark indicated that 98 percent of sales executives feel that mobile devices are essential to their selling success.

Research from the Aberdeen Group revealed that best-in-class companies were more likely to use sales tools than their average or lagging counterparts. Executives in 63 percent of the top-performing sales organizations actively support budgeting for and implementation of sales tools. Salespeople who use sales tools attribute increased sales success to the tools. Despite that evidence has shown that sales tools increase sales capacity, only 20 percent of sales forces

> *"Do more, reach further with less."*
> —Dinesh Dhamija,
> SVP and Chief
> Strategy Officer, TCDI

are using cutting-edge sales tools. In a Richardson survey of 500 diverse business-to-business (B2B) salespeople, 47 percent reported they did not actively use sales tools. Clearly these figures will change quickly as sales tools become even more essential to being competitive.

The right sales tools will enable you to get your job done better and faster. They will save you time and increase your sales capacity. CSO Insights and the Aberdeen Group reported that salespeople spend about 25 percent of their time researching prospects and looking for sales intelligence. Sales tools could reduce this to a low, single-digit number—as low as 1 percent. What would that mean to the quality of your preparation and productivity and your ability to expand relationships?

And if saving and increasing your time with clients isn't enough of a reason, sales tools improve the quality of your conversations. For example, tools such as Google Alerts, InsideView, LeadLander, Apple KeyNote, and OneSource monitor client trigger events and give you a heads up on emerging client needs such as a regulatory or management change. With early information you can quickly and proactively capitalize on opportunities by bringing insights and ideas to clients. You can raise the level of the dialogue with strategic questions and not bog down the conversation with questions you should know the answers to.

Sales tools give you (and your clients) sales mobility and untether you from your office. They keep you connected and give you the capacity to work remotely; for example, you can get access to material and create and change proposals when traveling. Video conferencing tools such as GoToMeeting, WebEx, and Skype simulate interactive face-to-face contact and can be a point of differentiation from your competitors who rely only on phone communication. Of course, utilizing video conferencing tools necessitates learning some etiquette, for example gaining the client's agreement for you to appear on camera, inviting your client to do the same, and thanking clients who agree. Mobile apps such as Kayak, which is used for checking or booking flights, provide vertical searches that save you time by bypassing other searches.

Things are changing fast, but many organizations, including technology companies, still are not fully leveraging technology. There are companies that are turning to their marketing teams and sales ops to develop knowledge-sharing engines that provide their sales forces with relevant information and insights to understand trends, meet the needs that are on clients' agendas, and anticipate future needs. Tools should be integrated based on an overall plan as a part of the sales workflow. Ideally your organization is among the fast moving companies, but even without support from corporate, many sales tools and resources are available to you—as they are to your competitors.

If sales tools are not on your or your sales leader's radar as a way to decrease non-selling time, increase time with clients, and improve the quality and outcome of calls, raise the topic.

But if you don't have corporate support, you can't wait for it. Many sales tools are free or inexpensive, and you can use them independent of your organization. Of course, collaboration and knowledge-sharing tools require leadership endorsement for funds to purchase, maintain, and update. Without collaboration tools efforts are unnecessarily duplicated and knowledge such as immediate access to client and industry information, ideas, answers to questions, product knowledge, competitive data, success stories, presentations, and insights is not shared. Sales organizations literally leave money on the table when they don't share what they learn from their successes and failures.

Because of the number of tools available, identifying the few among the hundreds that will make you more successful is a challenge. Without question the volume of information, tools, and apps can be overwhelming. Nonetheless, sorting through the maze to get the right tools when and where you need them is more than worth the effort.

To help you choose the tools that are right for you, consider the following points:

- Think about the most important things you must get accomplished each day.

- Identify a niche where you want to develop expertise.

- Figure out where your stumbling blocks are.

- Check out websites such as Smart Sales Tools to help you choose the tools you need, whether to help you develop a proposal, schedule an appointment, or build business acumen.

If your customer relationship management (CRM) software is your only sales tool, keep in mind that the basic concept of CRM software is more than 30 years old. Choose tools that integrate with your CRM.

Let's consider some of the tools that are available to you and how you can use them to help you reach your goals. Because of the speed at which technology is changing, some of the tools I mention in this chapter will be obsolete in the next few months and next-generation tools will take their place. Change is everywhere, as evidenced by Gartner Inc.'s prediction that by 2017 tablets will replace computers and laptops.

Here are just a few sales tools that can give you an edge:

- TimeTrade enables you to schedule appointments effortlessly in 30 seconds or less, and faster scheduling means more time for selling.

- Lead411 provides client addresses, business e-mail, and executive e-mail addresses and phone numbers.

- NetProspect was voted the most accurate business-to-business (B2B) contact information software.

- SalesQuest tracks the Fortune 1000 and Global 500 to help you look at your clients' current and future goals.

- CRUSH Reports is a high-end, expensive tool that provides complete analysis on Fortune 1000 companies from financials to e-mail addresses, and the free tool called CRUSHarmy enables you to download names of contacts for the accounts you want to crack into and to share leads based on a motivational point system.

- Google Maps provides driving directions to find local businesses.

- iSell lets you quickly identify names of clients to call and what to say based on relevance and sales triggers (an event that causes a client to identify and prioritize solving a problem), and it automatically prioritizes prospects to cut research time.

- Docusign lets you obtain a client's signature electronically to save time and avoid steps such as overnight packages, converting documents, and missing signatures. It cuts the average contract signing time from two days to less than an hour.

- iMeet enables you to lead online video meetings and connect with clients by simply having them enter the URL of the meeting room at which point the tool automatically dials the client's phone. Because software is not downloaded you reduce time and hassle.

- Incite2 is a collaboration tool that with a click can provide you with almost instant access to product knowledge, questions to ask, etc.

- Bloomfire is another collaboration tool that enables your company to share best practices such as proposals and templates and allows you and your colleagues to vote the materials up or down so the best ones rise to the top.

- Datahugs is a lead-generation tool that enables you to automatically pinpoint who knows whom and how they know them across your company's entire network of connections by scanning contact information in e-mails—no data entry necessary.

- Hubspot creates an all-in-one marketing solution for your company to generate leads. It takes the best of inbound marketing methods, tweets, and blogs, consolidating this disconnected stream of information into one spot to save time and increase results.

- HootSuite is a social media dashboard that allows your company to connect multiple social networks from one website to launch marketing campaigns, identify and grow audiences, and distribute targeted messages.

- Mobile video calling tools include Tango, Apple's FaceTime (a selling point for its iPad), Yahoo's OnTheAir, Microsoft's Skype (for both video and audio-only calls), Google Plus (200 aps for video calling feature), Hangouts (free video service for two- to ten-person video calls), and the independent service called Zoom that offers an app that works on Macs, Windows-based PCs, iPhones, and IPads at no cost for groups of up to 15 participants. These tools save travel time and money but more importantly add a visual connection to any phone call to allow you to differentiate yourself from your competitors.

- Presentation and video tools include YouTube (video sharing and a great credentialing tool), Brainshark (online and mobile presentations), and Snagit (pick up and share an image).

- iPads and tablets are incredibly useful in increasing productivity. For example, they enable you to easily demonstrate products or connect to your CRM software to check or change a schedule, download client information, share information with clients or teammates, take pictures as needed, and transmit data (iPad 2). Configure price quote (CPQ) tools streamline the purchase and quote process by eliminating paper-based quotes, which are error prone and time consuming.

■ Salesforce.com offers a range of powerful tools, such as Chatter.

■ Apps for managers and salespeople, such as Salespod, enable sales managers to manage and coach salespeople, manage clients, and capture information in real time.

Sales tools facilitate getting your job done faster, anywhere, anytime—whether building industry or competitive knowledge or learning something new about a long-term client or prospect before returning a call.

Just as clients have instant access to information that has made them smarter, you have the same access to data and tools to prepare you to drive results with insights and ideas to help clients anticipate and solve problems. Sites such as InsideView, LinkedIn, and Twitter are tools that enable you to see what clients, their competitors, and your own competitors are doing on a minute-by-minute basis in order to capitalize on opportunities as soon as they present themselves—or even create opportunities.

LinkedIn

With over 200 million members, LinkedIn stands out as the top social media tool. Next in line are Twitter (find out what your clients are saying and who they follow), Facebook, Pinterest (instantly clip pictures), and blogs. Use LinkedIn to:

■ Conduct research on prospects and clients leverage advanced search.

■ Connect to your target clients by sending a personal invite before making a phone call.

■ Share links, track interest, and connect with contacts.

■ Sift through connections quickly to build and rekindle relationships.

■ Build industry and client knowledge, for example through the groups you join.

- ■ Keep yourself abreast of hot issues.

- ■ Develop insights.

- ■ Create a presence.

- ■ Help clients know you from a personal and professional perspective.

Social media is powerful because it facilities client-to-client conversations and gives clients to have a loud voice. And that voice is a source of insights into the problems, opportunities, successes, and concerns they are talking about. According to Nielsen, users spend more time on social media than any other category of websites. Research by Jim Keenan and Barbara Giamanco showed that 72.6 percent of salespeople using social media outperformed their peers and exceeded quotas 23 percent more often. These salespeople are using social media to network, prospect, and conduct research. It enables social selling where your competency is vital. If you are not actively using social media, the evidence indicates that you should start doing so immediately. Sites such as Google offers free workshops.

Gaining knowledge is step one, but what you do with that knowledge to anticipate and solve your clients' challenges is what matters. Anyone can find almost any kind of knowledge easily and inexpensively; it is applying the knowledge that brings value. For example, Nancy uses Jigsaw as an integral part of her prospecting. She was able to act fast when she received an alert that a prospect had hired a new SVP of sales. The company had aggressive sales goals in emerging markets. Using LinkedIn she realized that the new SVP's experience came from outside the industry. She leveraged a second connection and sent a request to connect with the SVP. She followed that with a short e-mail to congratulate him on the position, request a meeting, and summarize her awareness of the strategic and growth goals. She also included information about her company's extensive relevant industry experience. She offered to connect the SVP with one of her clients. The following day she left a voice mail message. The SVP responded to her e-mail to arrange a phone conversation that led to a sale.

The resources available will make you more successful if you consistently tap into them. For example, Nigel Edelshain reported that by researching and connecting with a prospect through LinkedIn as a second connection, a salesperson is 30 percent more likely to connect—versus 5 percent with e-mail—and more likely to make a quality conversation happen. InsideeView reported that 90 percent of executives don't ever respond to cold calls, yet they almost always return a call when the referral is a trusted colleague.

> *"We are on the tail end of technology being special. The automobile was a weird technology when it first debuted, then after a while, it evolved and designers stepped in to add value to it."*
> —John Meade, President, Rhode Island School of Design

Summary

Clients have a filter that quickly tells them how prepared you are and whether you will create value for them. In the past clients were more tolerant and patient when it came to educating you. Their willingness to fill in the blanks regarding things you could have or should have known is a thing of the past. You are expected to know everything you possibly can based on the resources available to you in order to get your clients' attention and earn time with them.

Whether you use the Sales Ready Tool (please see Appendix) or a tool provided by your organization, meta-prepare as a core competency. One of the worst sales managers I worked with told his employees, "Don't waste time researching your prospects. Just use the script." There is little wonder why his team was not succeeding. One of the most highly successful sales leaders I worked with draped a banner across the front of the sales seminar room with the words "No Surprises." He aimed to have his salespeople as close to 360 degrees prepared as possible for every client conversation.

Old world tools were limited by the discipline and motivation of the salesperson and what he or she entered into a client file. This information was then made available to just one or two people and rarely leveraged. Beyond speed and immediacy for each salesperson, sales tools make populating and sharing data with team members across divisions, geographies, and clients possible. They cultivate connections. They put knowledge into the workflow and embed collaboration into the culture.

Before you meet with your client, do your research to understand the key challenges in the client's industry and business. By becoming industry, company, and stakeholder ready, you will create a competitive edge that will enable you to produce results for your clients and yourself. Use social media to understand how your clients think, buy, and act. Pay attention to what they say and who they listen to. Select the sales tools that will help you build your knowledge and increase your productivity. What passed for preparation just a short time ago no longer makes the grade. Knowing about your clients before you speak with them is a *must do*, not a *nice to do*. Table 1.1 contains a side-by-side look at how values have shifted during recent years.

> "Almost nothing . . . can scale as quickly, efficiently, or aggressively as technology platforms, and this makes the people who build, control, and use them powerful too."
> —Eric E. Schmidt, Executive Chairman, Google

Table 1.1 The New Approach to Gaining Knowledge

From	To
■ Features and benefits	■ Risk and value
■ Products	■ Business challenges
■ Product solutions	■ Business outcomes
■ Product knowledge expertise	■ Company and stakeholder expertise
■ Functional boundaries	■ Functional alignment
■ Product differentiation	■ Salesperson differentiation
■ Discovery-driven questions	■ Insight- and idea-driven questions
■ Price	■ Proof
■ Risk	■ Surety
■ Responding	■ Creating and shaping
■ Pitching	■ Collaborative teaching
■ Satisfying department needs	■ Incorporating corporate strategy
■ Buyer approval	■ Cross-functional consensus
■ Sales process	■ Client buying cycle
■ CRM	■ CRM, integrated sales-enablement tools, and apps

3

Heat-Mapping: Anticipating Client Needs

"Knowing a client persona is not the same as knowing *the* client."

"Questions are more persuasive than telling."

D
ata from Forrester showed that a scant 19 percent of clients rate their conversations with salespeople as valuable. This finding underscores the need for most salespeople to think twice about the conversations they are having with their clients.

Buyers have made it clear that they are tired of product pitches. It is worth repeating that the Corporate Executive Board study showed decision makers are as much as 57 percent through their buying cycle before engaging with salespeople. And there is no question the majority of these self-educating clients are using social media to get input from their peers. It is now a given that clients are doing their homework, leveraging social media, and talking with their team members and colleagues to figure out how to solve their business challenges. Because clients have advanced in their buying cycle and know—or at least think they know—what they want to accomplish and the options available to them *before* they talk to you, it is crucial for you to demonstrate very early on in a meeting that you know their world and can add to what they already know. At the same time, there remains information you must gather to be fully relevant.

Heat-mapping is the term I use to describe the new need dialogue to underscore that because of the changes in clients' buying habits, the need dialogue, while still critical, no longer can be confined to discovery questions. A heat map uses color at a glance to make it easier and faster to understand data; for example, red and blue colors on a map during a U.S. election to distinguish between Republicans and Democrats. In a similar way, heat-mapping sales uses insights and knowledge to turn up the heat and raise the visibility of a business challenge where you believe you can bring value to your client. When you heat map, you use an insight or knowledge to engage a client and open up a need dialogue that explores a priority business challenge and works backward to a solution.

The question is *how* to share that insight or knowledge. There is a school of thought that recommends taking a "knowier than thou" approach of walking in and telling clients what they don't know and what they should do. The problem with that approach is that the content you are sharing is based is an assumption, an educated guess—until tested. Moreover, how many of your clients, especially in the C-suite, respond well to being told what to do and what they don't know? Indeed, clients are hungry for relevant insights and ideas that broaden their perspectives and forestall and help solve business problems. They highly value frank, open, and honest dialogues. But they want you to communicate *with* them, not only to them. All the content you work so hard to build up in futuring is best paired with informed questions in a collaborative heat-mapping dialogue.

While clients are under pressure to perform and expect insights and ideas, they too have expertise and experience. They demand to be recognized and respected. It is true that clients have little patience for educating you on issues they have already thought through or that they expect you to already understand. They won't answer a long list of uninformed discovery questions. They are suffering from questioning fatigue. On the one hand, you must to be ready from the first conversation to demonstrate you know their business and can bring value. At the same time, however, you must elicit information to go from a generalized insight to something that is really relevant and persuasive.

The saving grace is that clients intuitively know that no matter how much expertise you have about their business, industry, or them, you can't know how they see their world or what is unique about their situation or them, and that you must get information from them. Even with the very best client analytics, research, and deep experience there

> *"In the new world questions can have more impact than answers. We are living in the age of the client."*
> —Joel Anderson, CEO, Walmart.com

are things such as corporate or divisional strategy, point of view, ideas already considered or in the works or rejected, hard-to-uncover politics, ingrained personal biases, financial issues, and personal goals that are rarely available through research or experience. Clients are not interchangeable. No two decisions are ever exactly the same. Even if two different clients seem to have exactly the same needs, they can think differently about them. Moreover, almost all clients see themselves as unique. Clients want to be a part of the revelation and the solutions, not the recipients. Unless you can read minds, and even if you can, there is no escaping the need to make clients contributors. It is the combination of insights and questions that is one of the distinguishing marks of the new sales conversations. The big difference in the structure and content of the questions.

Questioning isn't the culprit. But a list of discovery questions in search of a product opportunity, once so effective, is a problem. Clients will participate gladly when questions are informed and they see a payoff because the questions are directed toward solving a priority business challenge. Asking the right questions at the right time to the right people can be as, and often more, educational and persuasive as offering insights and answers. Stephen Shapiro, author of *Best Practices Are Stupid*, pointed out that people remember ideas more easily when they are phrased as questions than when they are presented as answers. Clearly a new conversation is needed, and the questions you ask and how you ask them are a big part of the change.

> *"They (tenured Disney artists) were the masters of form but they had the attitude of students. . . . The masters were never satisfied. When the new head of animations said 'I am satisfied with what I do,' he lost me."*
> —Brad Bird, genius behind Pixar's films

New Times, New Questions

Like most salespeople you have probably been schooled to ask questions before you present ideas. Consultative selling and other client need–based selling methodologies have questioning at their heart. Over the past few decades salespeople have been encouraged to engage clients by probing—and many have become adept at it. But the way your clients buy has evolved, and so must consultative selling and how you probe.

Just as there are new technical sales tools, there are data and new questioning skills that build on and often replace typical discovery questions so much a part of need dialogues in the past. Insights play a big role in the new sales conversation. When you combine an insight with a question, you form an *insight-led question* that both gives and takes. By giving and taking you solve the dilemma of demonstrating that you can bring value to your clients early in the conversation and at the same time gain the information you need. Insight-led questions are a hybrid in that *before you ask them you share relevant insights or knowledge as a lead into the probe.*

Whether you bring an insight, knowledge, or ideas to a client in response to a need your client has already identified or one in which you create an awareness, there is almost always information about the client that you must gather. The director of product management for Google's real-time communications, Nikhyl Singhal, reinforced the need to go beyond generalizations about customers to understand the preferences of the individual to help Google sell more ads: "Google works better when we know who you are and what your interests are."

Of course, sharing insights is not new to selling or probing. But it has never been common. Top performers have differentiated themselves from average performers in large part by bringing deeper expertise, insights, and ideas to their clients. But that level of value can no longer be the province of only the top performers. The bad news is that there is little room for average performers on the new sales map.

Today the easy sales are being taken to the Internet. The Internet has further separated the complex and transactional sale by moving the transactional sale online. In the transactional sale clients are less dependent on salespeople for expertise. Transactional clients fundamentally know what they want and are usually able to implement on their own. Research by Neil Rackham showed that just a few years ago the transactional–consultative sales continuum formed a bell curve. His study showed that there were many clients in the middle who were a combination of the consultative (needing a certain amount of advice) and transactional (needing little or no support) buyer. That middle group usually had an understanding of their needs but were willing to pay a limited amount for support, customization, and execution. The gap between the consultative and transactional sale has grown larger, and the center will soon disappear along with the role of the average performer. But that does not mean the predictions about "death of a salesman" are true. If you turn the bell curve upside down, you get a smile. In fact there may well be fewer salespeople overall and a merging of face-to-face and phone selling. However high-level salespeople will be in greater demand than ever—and in shorter supply. Average salespeople will struggle to be relevant to the new buyer and the complex sale.

While the interrogative call is over, the consultative, collaborative call is not—but it has advanced. An insight and knowledge sharing dump is no better than a product dump.

Insights and questioning now go hand in hand. The sharing of an insight is the starting point because insights are probabilities, not certainties. Therefore, it is important when you share insights to follow insights with questions in order to (1) test how relevant the insight is *to the client*, (2) gain the client's perspective and experience, (3) lead into exploring the business challenge related to the insight so you can customize your idea, and (4) communicate *with* (not *to*) your client. With insight-led questions the insights show you bring an understanding of an issue, problem, or opportunity, spark new thinking, and create a reason for clients to consider engaging and changing. In its highest form the insight *teaches clients something they don't know.*

Not all insights *create* awareness. Some *shape* clients' thinking by adding a different perspective about an issue on their radar. In either case you plant a seed of dissatisfaction with the status quo and you earn the right to probe the issue.

While it is true that clients in the same industries and in the same roles share common issues, the question that follows the insight is as important as the insight itself. The Greek philosopher Heraclitus summed it up with his observation, "A person never steps into the same river twice." How they think is unique. Is the client analytical, creative, open-minded? Without probing your clients' perceptions at every important juncture, you risk going down the wrong path or creating an impression of arrogance. Without probing, the only answers you have are the ones you walked in with. By combining insights and questions, you go in smart and leave smarter.

Meaningful insights:

- Are relevant: They center on a business challenge or opportunity that you believe is a priority for the client.

- Teach or provide a new perspective: They create awareness of an issue the client is not aware of or shape how the client looks at an issue already on his or her agenda.

- Drive to your strength: They relate to a problem or missed opportunity you can solve.

- Are backed up with data: They include data, experience, and examples to validate financial impact.

■ Often create contrast: They compare a more advantageous alternative with the current or more commmon approach.

■ Are objective: They present the pros and cons in an unbiased teacher–advisor versus sales manner. David Ramsey, respected financial advisor, recently gave this council to his TV audience: "When you want advice about investing, go to a teacher (academia), not a salesman."

■ Elicit feedback: They seek the client's perspective or experience by asking, "What has your experience been with this? What is your perspective in regard to this?"

■ Are brief: They can be presented in two to three minutes at most.

For example:

A study by . . . showed that patient eye health, satisfaction, and compliance increase by . . . percent when patients use two-week contact lenses as compared with one-month lenses. With the two-week lenses patients report . . . improvement. This is in contrast to . . . in which . . . problems exist. Additionally the transition to two-week lenses has a positive financial impact on the practices that have made the change and have increased their revenue by . . . Two-week lenses also reduced the number of return visits to refit lenses by 45 percent. What has your experience been with your one-month lenses?

There are variations of insight-led questions that help clients reconsider their current situation and look at issues in a new way. *Insightful questions* put a sharper lens on a problem by helping a client focus on what is essential and cut through all the noise. Peter Drucker, management guru, was the master of insightful questions. He taught by using insights in the form of Socratic questions to help his clients look at their world in a new way and to cut through all the noise. For example, rather than give a CEO reasons to divest or not divest a company, he would ask an insightful question that heat mapped what the client should think about, such as, "If you didn't own this company, would you buy it now?" *Informed questions* are another way to teach by asking a knowledge-driven question that the client had not yet considered. For example, Charlie took business from an incumbent when he discovered a hole in a policy: "Thanks for sharing your policy with me to review. I see the coverage for [x and y] are comprehensive. In working with . . . we found gaps in . . . which caused . . . How does that coverage work for transport, which I know is a growing part of your business?" Another kind of informed question is a trading question in which you set up an exchange of information: "We are seeing a trend across the industry to use . . . technology to help sales teams tell their story. . . . For example one of our large pharmaceutical clients has armed its global sales force and technical support with . . . as compared with . . . Our client reported an increase in revenue of . . . With the launch of your new product this coming quarter, what thoughts have you given to using technology to support your engineers in their new client contact role?"

Sharing insights as a part of questioning raises the level of the dialogue, but this approach is not without pitfalls. Be careful to avoid these traps:

- Starting with good intentions but moving into a telling mode too quickly without exploring the client's perspective on the challenge
- Coming across as arrogant
- Being focused on yourself rather than the client
- Being irrelevant

While you are formulating client insights, your clients too are arriving at their own insights as they conduct research and network. They may even say, "Tell me what to do." But they won't likely be moved by your insight or buy into your recommendations if they don't feel ownership. When clients ask, "Any advice?" it means they trust you. It is an invitation to add value and explore possibilities *together*. Whether it is an opportunity you create or one you respond to, whether it is a client you have reached out to or an Internet lead, insights will help you gain clients' interest. Insights enrich, not replace, the interactive need dialogue.

Modes of Selling

It is important to understand where you are in your client's buying cycle because that affects your level of influence and your client's expectations. There are three primary modes of selling based on where you enter the client's buying cycle. The three modes of selling are: create the opportunity, shape the opportunity, and respond to the opportunity.

Creating the Opportunity

This is the most proactive mode of selling. In the create mode you bring an insight or idea to a client to raise his or her awareness of a challenge or opportunity that is *not yet on the radar*. You create demand for a solution you believe your client needs and you can provide. You get to clients before they are in the market, and therefore you place yourself in a strong position to influence their objectives, decision-making criteria, scope of the initiative, and budget.

In the create mode you can often circumvent the request for proposal (RFP) process. You serve as teacher, coach, and advisor. It is increasingly difficult to persuade clients based on product and price, but by bringing insights and relevant ideas to clients when they are not yet in the market, you create an advisor role.

When you are in the create mode you disrupt the client's status quo. Not surprisingly, many clients resist changing systems that seem to be working. But clients also value frankness and want to be alerted to potential issues and spared from being blindsided. Moreover, it is your responsibility to give them your best advice even when it may not be what you think they want to hear.

As covered earlier it is critical to explore the insight with your client to avoid turning the insight into an in-fight.

Possible downsides to creating opportunities are: (1) the risk of kissing a lot of frogs, (2) starting early and raising the cost of the sale, (3) ruffling feathers, and (4) being able to successfully engage with executives at a strategic level. But the benefits when executed well far outweigh these concerns. The key is to carefully qualify the opportunities to focus your efforts where you will have the best chance of winning and rely on your sales process and verifiable outcomes (see Chapter 5) to help you develop a realistic assessment of each opportunity.

A manager of operations in a manufacturing company summed up the high value she places on salespeople who bring insights and ideas when she said, "There are a lot of salespeople who can sell you a ladder after you have fallen into a hole but few who can prevent you from falling in." Even if your client doesn't buy into the insight or idea you bring, you benefit by learning more and positioning yourself in the role of thought partner.

Shaping the Opportunity

Clients are smart. So it's not surprising that they are identifying challenges before or at the same time as you are. But you can still add value and create a competitive advantage by helping them look at a priority challenge in a new way. The earlier you can intercept the opportunity, the easier it is to influence the buying decision.

Responding to the Opportunity

When clients don't require any added value or when they are so far along in understanding their needs that they have settled on a solution, you likely will be in an order-taking or fulfillment role. In this mode you can have the least impact and control, and clients view you and pay you as a commodity. You must recognize legitimate opportunities to respond as such and appropriately manage the effort and resources you dedicate to them.

Depending on how advanced clients are in their buying cycle and how much value you bring in the form of insights, ideas, consulting, or support in execution, it is possible to convert a respond opportunity into a shape or even create opportunity. For example, based on your expertise you may find a way to add value by expanding the scope of an RFP, redefining the need, changing the decision criteria, adding to or subtracting elements of the solution, or even changing the direction completely. The good news is that most clients place high value on salespeople who suggest changes they believe will help them succeed. For example, you can expand the client's thinking and build a better solution by saying something like this:

> I've carefully reviewed your RFP and appreciate your considering us. Thanks for the meeting to learn more about your initiative. I understand the impact an initiative like this can have on staff productivity. One of our large retail clients in . . . also went through cutbacks to . . . It was critical they . . . We helped them reduce the time it took to optimize store-specific pricing from 30 to 2 hours to reduce . . . and resulted in a 4 percent increase in staff productivity. Cutbacks are one of the challenges you identified in the RFP. Based on our . . . . we find that a critical element to achieving . . . is . . . but this was not included in your RFP. I would like to understand your thinking on this. . . . We would like to build that into our proposal. What are your thoughts on our including . . . ?

Think about the opportunities in your pipeline. Which selling modes dominate? If you are like most salespeople, your challenge is to find ways to *create* more opportunities. By relying heavily on responding to opportunities, you place yourself in a long line of competitors. You set yourself up for price pressure. Of course, there will always be a mix of the three selling modes in your pipeline, but the goal is to increase the percentage of create opportunities to give you the full client buying cycle to influence the scope of the initiative and decision criteria (see Figure 3.1).

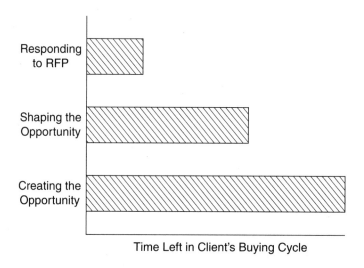

Time Left in Client's Buying Cycle

What is the current mix in your pipeline?

Creating opportunities   _____%

Shaping opportunities   _____%

Responding to opportunities   _____%

Figure 3.1 Your Opportunity to Shape and Influence the Client's Decision

Great Selling Is Great Teaching

There is an element of teaching in sharing insights. So what is the most effective teaching methodology to engage your clients? We have all had good teachers and bad teachers. In a 2012 survey by the Center for Learning Technologies and the Social Learning Center, 90 percent of respondents cited collaboration as the most essential element for learning. This finding has implications for educating clients.

There has been a fundamental change in how clients learn, and it has carried over to how they buy. We are in an era of collaboration. Clients are using analytics, Google searches, as well as personal and professional networks, communities, and blogs to broaden their thinking. They respond well to collaboration. They want answers but not presented from on high. They want to learn. They want to learn fast. They want to learn from you. But they have knowledge and egos, and they want to be contributors to the learning. They want collaborative dialogues.

New Need Dialogue Models and Skills

An effective model visually depicts the steps needed to execute something. It provides an approach that works and is repeatable. A need dialogue model gives you a cadence for planning, asking questions, and eliciting the answers you need.

Before the age of the Internet, the questioning cadence that most effective salespeople used looked like this: probe, listen, acknowledge . . . probe, listen, acknowledge. This discovery process aimed at identifying needs. Of course some insights were interjected into the process, but the key objective was to probe to understand client needs related to product solutions.

In the old cadence most effective salespeople uncovered client needs by first asking a broader, more strategic question to better understand a client's objectives, whether it was a need the client had identified or one the salesperson introduced. The subsequent questions primarily centered on finding a fit between the need and the salesperson's offering. Once the objective was understood, the salesperson moved on to probe current practices—what was and was not working, what the client wanted to change, stakeholders, technical and future needs, personal drivers, and implementation information such as time frame, compelling event, and budget—that were relevant to their product solution.

The client and product probing and need discovery model belongs to yesterday. The importance of changing this model is underscored in the Forrester study, which showed that clients believe 45 percent of salespeople probe until they identify a product need (i.e., hear a buzzword) and quickly take that as their cue to talk about (i.e., pitch) their products.

While there is a place for traditional product-related discovery questions, those questions are asked later in the dialogue. The timing of asking those questions has changed. By positioning the insight and exploring the business challenge first you open up a conversation at the business rather than product level.

As high as 50 percent of sales opportunities result in *no decision*. Of course there are multiple reasons why salespeople lose deals either to a competitor or to a no decision. While salespeople often attribute the loss of the opportunity to price or their having an inferior product—and at times these are truly the cause—client feedback often points to other factors. Too often clients report they are not convinced that the gain outweighs the risk and therefore are not moved to change the status quo. How many times has a client said to you, "My job is on the line"? With that mindset it can feel safer to do nothing.

To develop winning solutions starts with knowing your clients business and personal needs at a granular level. Your goal is to get the answers to questions such as these:

- What is the business challenge?

- Why should this client change? Why now?

- What is the negative impact of remaining with the status quo?

- What would the improved situation look like? What is the outcome?

- Why should the client make the change with me?

- How will I differentiate my solution?

- How will I prove value?

- Who are the stakeholders?

- Who is the executive sponsor?

- What are the current costs?

- What are the ongoing costs?

- What are the personal motivations and preferences?

- What other priorities is the client focusing on?

- What are the politics?

- What is the compelling event?

New Need Dialogue Models

The new need dialogue models will help you move your conversations from product to business outcome and gain the information you need to build a winning solution. They are as much a sales tool as LinkedIn or Jigsaw.

There are two need dialogue models, and they are slightly different based on whether you are creating or shaping and responding to an opportunity.

You will notice there are multiple parts to each model. Clients are sophisticated in their decision making. Mobilizing them to act requires that you understand all of the priorities on all key stakeholders' checklists.

The two new need dialogue models are:

- *Create the Opportunity Model*—Use this model when you are *raising a client's awareness* of a need or opportunity that is not on his or her radar.

- *Shape and Respond to the Opportunity Model*—Use this model when your *client is already aware of a need.* This model is similar to the create model except in the opening statement. Because the issue is already on the client's agenda, acknowledge the client's focus and probe to learn more about how the client perceives the issue.

Create the Opportunity Need Dialogue Model

There are five parts to this model: position the insight (two to three minutes), position high level of idea (two to three minutes), explore the business challenge, explore the opportunity (full need dialogue), and next steps.

Position the Insight

- Position the challenge (e.g., "One of the key issues we are seeing is . . ." "Research from . . . shows that 25 percent of . . ." "There is a growing trend . . . 10 percent fewer . . .").

- Share the insight.

- Position your point of view.

- Support with research and ROI.

- Show relevance to client.

- Compare and contrast typical approach with alternative (e.g., "Instead it is possible to . . .") and describe associated risk (e.g., "The downside . . .").

- Probe for client's experience and perception.

Position High Level of the Idea

- Connect to solving business challenge.

- Provide a success story.

- Check for client reaction (e.g., "What do you think of . . . ?").
  - If agreement go to Explore the Business Challenge.
  - If disagreement probe to understand why.

Explore the Business Challenge

- Identify desired outcome.

- Determine the factors that must be in place to achieve the outcome (e.g., "What would have to be in place?").

- Identify the stakeholders involved (e.g., "Who from your organization would be involved and/or affected?").

- Establish current costs and ongoing costs.

Explore the Opportunity

- Probe objective.

- Understand the current situation and level of satisfaction.

- Explore technical needs.

- Establish future needs.

- Review implementation issues.

- Determine personal drivers.

Next Steps

- Ask questions to help client internalize the idea (e.g., "How do you think this approach would work here?" "What obstacles might arise?" "What would prompt action?").

- Check for questions.

- Gain agreement for next step, and ask for access to stakeholders.

Let's look at the key elements of the model in more depth.

Raise the Challenging Issue

Introduce the issue that you want to discuss in an objective and neutral way. For example, "We have been closely following the innovations made in China to use recycled paper . . . and the pressure that is placing on the paper industry to find new ways to . . . When . . . is applied the costs can be reduced by X percent . . . and production increased by Y percent . . ." Ask the client to share his or her experience or perception.

Share Your Insight

Position your prepared insight to begin to make a case for change. Teach with a balanced view; don't pitch. The insight you share will challenge the status quo, and therefore it is important to provide data, experience, and examples of the financial impact to gain the client's interest. Communicate the contrast between the alternative and the current or typical approach. Focus your client on the risks associated with maintaining the status quo and the measurable benefits of making a change. Probe the client's view. (See Appendix for Insight Statement Template.)

Position High Level of the Idea and Teach Alternative Approach

Position the high level of your idea and support it with a brief success story and example of ROI. Tell the client how it works. Ask for feedback from the client to gauge whether there is sufficient interest to pursue further.

Explore the Challenge and the Opportunity

Ask strategic and informed questions to understand the objectives, desired outcome, stakeholders, current and ongoing costs, missed opportunity, current situation, potential obstacles, stakeholders, and so on.

Set Next Steps

Gauge the client's interest in making a change. Set an action step. Request access to stakeholders and the executive who would be involved in making the decision. Develop a follow-up strategy to continue to develop interest in the idea and maintain momentum. If there is an opportunity to broaden the conversation, continue the dialogue. Usually there will be multiple conversations with multiple stakeholders before you are ready to move from idea to solution and/or customized recommendation. When you are fully prepared to make your recommendation, use the Value Solution Model (see Chapter 4).

Let's explore how Terri used the model to create an opportunity. As a part of her call preparation she learned from the utility company's website that its eight divisions operated as separate units. Based on her industry knowledge she knew it was likely that the company's data was held in multiple places, making it time consuming to consolidate information and slowing response in a time of crisis. She succeeded in getting the meeting with the COO, but not by touting her product or by asking product-related questions. Instead she raised the business challenge. She shared an insight, gained the COO's perspective, and focused on the challenge of improving response time in a time of crisis. Here is a breakdown of her process:

■ "I mentioned in our phone call . . . I appreciate the opportunity to meet today to share the . . . research and learn about your priorities. I understand that a system outage is a crisis that can always be around the corner . . . difficult issues of safety and public relations. The . . . research study shows that by combining data more quickly it is possible to gain a critical time advantage of two to three hours to respond to or even avert a crisis. In our experience we have found . . . with clients such as . . . those critical hours saved significantly and reduced the chance of injury or damage as compared to . . . I know how important . . . is and . . . the impact of . . . I would like to understand what *your experience* has been with response time."

■ "What are your objectives for your team in terms of responding in a time of crisis? What would be the desired outcome?"

■ "What would *have to be in place across the organization* for that to happen?"

■ "Who among the team would be affected by . . . ? What process is followed in making a decision (e.g., identify economic decision maker, executive, influencers, and users, and identify political alignment, for example who is ally, coach, detractor, neutral)?"

■ "In working with . . . we found by . . . savings of . . . compared to . . . What *costs* do you attach to . . . for your organization? What are the costs to your clients?"

Once she understood the business challenge, she probed the opportunity with questions such as:

■ "Your website mentioned eight divisions. How are they organized . . .?"

■ "How does your current structure affect response time in a time of crisis?"

■ "The data from . . . showed that response time can be improved by . . . when the communication and processes among divisions . . . How do you currently combine the data from across your eight departments to coordinate your response?"

■ "How is that working? What challenges . . . ?"

■ "In working with . . . we found by . . . savings of . . . compared to . . . What *costs* do you attach to . . . for your organization? What are the costs to your clients?"

By presenting a meaningful insight and asking informed questions, Terri engaged the COO at the business challenge level, established her potential to help the client succeed, and gained the information she needed. After four meetings and multiple phone calls over a five-month period Terri closed a strategically important seven-figure sale and established a thought partner relationship with the COO.

Of course, you're not always solving business challenges at the strategic level. One savvy VP of sales at a technology company made that point when he said, "There needs to be a balance between knowing how your solution impacts the business and selling just what a client needs. If the client really just needs 'a line' then just sell the line!" At times this may be the case—unless by understanding why the client needs "a line" you can uncover a broader need and larger opportunity. The risk of just taking the order and selling "a line" is that your competitor may be providing advice, solving the root business challenge, and taking your business.

Dan turned a small opportunity into a $1.7 million opportunity by bringing an idea to his client. During a strategic account review Karen, Dan's sales manager, saw that he was competing for a small opportunity with a major financial institution. Dan's contacts were two midlevel managers, but the decision maker was the division executive. During a coaching session Karen shared an insight about a trend across financial institutions in which success was being measured by cost-efficiency ratios (percentage of overhead to revenue) in which each line of business is expected to make a contribution. With this knowledge and some coaching, Dan saw the potential for a much larger enterprise license with his client.

They strategized that Dan would inform his gatekeeper, the contact who had been blocking him from getting to the executive, that his sales manager and an SVP of Operations wanted to meet with the executive for a senior-to-senior meeting. He included his contact. Dan sent an e-mail to the executive in which he shared an insight regarding cost-efficiency ratios and asked for a meeting on behalf of his senior team and himself:

I have not had the pleasure of being formally introduced to you. I am the regional VP . . . and have been speaking with . . . regarding several small projects . . .

I know that many of our banking clients are looking for ways to improve efficiency ratios and that their . . . divisions are partnering with the LOBs more proactively to improve effectiveness and efficiency. Rather than . . . our team recently converted one of our longstanding U.S. banking clients to an enterprise license for all of the . . . which lowered their projected annual licensing spending with us by 16 percent.

In discussing your . . . we think there is a way to . . . My SVP of operations, my regional manager, and I would like to meet with you to understand your priorities and share with you our new . . . which we launched six months ago that has significantly reduced costs for our clients. We understand the constraints that the economy and new legislation have imposed on our financial services clients, and we are looking to proactively provide additional value . . . We would like to get your perspective on how . . . savings for you.

Would November 7th or Thursday November 8th be convenient for a meeting at your office? If this timing doesn't work, please suggest a time that would be convenient for you. We are looking forward to meeting with you. I will follow up with you on . . . .

On the same day the executive responded by e-mail accepting the invitation to meet. By bringing a relevant insight, supporting it with an actionable idea, and probing to understanding what was unique about the client's needs, two months after the meeting Dan closed on a $1.7 million licensing agreement and was positioned to continue to work with the executive and her team.

Shape the Opportunity Model

Throughout dialogue ask the questions that can be hard to ask, for example about competitors, obstacles, budget, metrics, and costs. Although you can research your competitors, only your clients can tell you how they rate each competitor and how they think you compare. Asking competitive questions doesn't only help you. It helps your clients recognize differences and weigh the value of their options. Clients are risk averse, and therefore you should probe to understand the risks they are assessing so you can mitigate the risks as much as possible in your solution. To understand what can lead to a no decision, ask, "What do you see as the biggest challenges to making a change such as this?" or "What challenges might come up in making a purchase like this?" Ask what metrics the client cares about. Is it higher profits; improved cash flow; greater earnings before interest, taxes, depreciation, and amortization (EBITDA); top-line growth; or something else? To show financial impact, ask questions to better understand current costs, for example, "So I may think about . . . , what are your current costs?" "How would you see this affecting your . . . ?" "If you don't move forward with this, what do you see as the possible downside?"

The purpose of the need dialogue is to understand what your clients want and what they value so you can truly tailor the content of your solution. While some sales methodologies minimize asking questions, many situations will in fact require that you ask more questions. The big difference is that the questions are a part of a business outcome—not product—dialogue, and you are at the table as a business equal. The catch with questioning is that you must have expertise and listen, which can also mean additional probing, modifying of *your* thinking, and in some situations going back to the drawing board.

The Shape the Opportunity model is similar to the Create the Opportunity model with the exception of the introductory part.

Because the challenge is already on the client's agenda, it is important to acknowledge the challenge (I know you are focused on . . . .) and explore the client's thinking about the challenge including why now and who is driving the initiative. Once you understand the driving issues, position your insight and continue to follow the Create the Opportunity Model.

Let's look at how Bill *shaped* an opportunity that began as an inquiry. An HR manager of a technology company, on behalf of her EVP of sales and service, sent an e-mail to Bill's company and to four of his competitors requesting a proposal for a coaching program for 33 sales managers to reduce sales force turnover. Before calling the HR manager, Bill quickly conducted research and learned that the company was a large, well-funded technology start-up. On the surface this sale could have been quick, profitable, and transactional.

But Bill's experience and expertise led him down a different path. Rather than probing at the product-need level with more traditional product-fit questions about objectives of the training, timing, and budget, Bill put insight-led questions to work. Initially the HR manager was adamant on a one-day coaching program, but when Bill shared an insight on turnover, probed her experience, and explored the business issues, the composition of the sales force, and the outcome the EVP wanted to achieve, he learned that only 10 percent of the sales force was hitting its numbers and that turnover was up to 100 percent in some territories.

Bill was the only competitor to request a call with the HR manager and the EVP to ensure that the initiative produced the results the EVP wanted. He shared insights with the EVP on recruiting sales managers from the pool of top producers, cultural fit, and the cost of sales force turnover. When he probed to find out about the composition of the sales force, he learned that they had been recruited from the two industry leaders. Based on his experience, he discussed how it was likely that in their former sales roles, they hadn't faced start-up company objections and had most likely not worked remotely. This struck a chord with the EVP, who confirmed that Bill's "hunches" were right. The EVP then opened up about the additional need to get the sales force to "sing from the same hymnbook."

The EVP knew that he had a need, but Bill reengineered the need and configured a solution that produced results. By sharing insights and asking informed questions Bill moved from a sales to an advisor role. He helped the EVP understand that coaching training was not in this situation the best place to start and recommended focusing first on reworking the hiring profile. Then he expanded the training beyond coaching to include messaging for the entire sales force. He put numbers to the cost of turnover and showed the impact of raising the number of salespeople reaching quota conservatively by 15 percent. The result was a win for all. Bill won the opportunity with a new long-term client, and the client made adjustments to his hiring practices and implemented a messaging and coaching program. After 10 months 70 percent of the sales force was reaching quota, and the sales force was stabilizing.

But what if, for example, you were Bill and the EVP or HR manager had persisted in wanting a quick fix that you believed would not likely produce the desired results? Expertise and probing are key here. *Your job is to confidently and respectfully find out why, and once you understand the client's perspective give your best advice*—supported with data that ties back to solving the business challenge. But when clients insist on following their path and you believe the solution they want is not ideal, unless it is unethical, illegal, or could be harmful to the client or your organization, the client has the final say. Whether or not your clients accept your recommendations, at the very least they will see you made a strong case and that you have their best interest at heart. Often, providing a less-than-ideal solution can be the first small step to a better solution in the future.

Of course, many sales opportunities are transactional, and the response mode is appropriate. However, it is important to ask questions to make sure you are not missing an opportunity to shape the need, add more value, and get paid for it. There is a lot of talk about "challenging" clients, but the challenge should not come at the outset of the conversation but as the outcome—when the clients reflect and realize the positive impact you have had on their thinking.

Keep the Need Conversation Interactive

A January 2012 article in the *Wall Street Journal* reinforced the need to not only teach clients but also ask questions and listen to understand what is unique about them. The lesson learned was simple: Engage with clients. Listen to them. Don't tell them—at least not until you know how they think. Doctors and their staffs are notorious for not wanting a sales pitch, but they are very open to learning.

Several of the large pharmaceutical firms found that their well-scripted approach in which they provided reps with a carefully customized message tailored to hospital groups, practices, and buyer roles was ineffective. They discovered that, although the scripts had been tailored to their clients' practices and personas, the reps were not equipped to "intuit and respond" to what individual clients actually wanted.

The carefully researched and tailored prescripted pitches seemed generic to clients. The reps were sharing insights but not engaging their clients. The firms found that sales performance improved and relationships grew stronger when they changed their strategy to one that placed emphasis on probing and listening to leverage insight and knowledge sharing. One firm reported an increase in sales of $450 million over its previous quarter once its sales force began to share insights, probe, and listen to its clients.

Probing Skills

It has often been said that if you want to get good answers, ask good questions. Although some clients are close to the vest, most clients, if they feel they can benefit, will share information. But even clients who are open often provide partial answers—not purposely but because they haven't thought the concepts through. Moreover, it is your job to ferret out the information you need. By preparing insight-led, insightful, and informed questions and developing your probing and listening skills you can help clients think issues through more fully convince themselves while you gather the essential information you need to differentiate your solution.

The content of your questions tells your clients your level of expertise. But how you ask questions also affects how they view you and respond. In addition to constructing insight-led questions, the following three questioning skills will help you elicit complete and insightful answers:

Acknowledgment and Empathy

Acknowledge or empathize what your client shares with you *before* you probe. This shows that you've listened, demonstrates respect for the client's point of view, and encourages the client to stay engaged and receptive. Acknowledgment is an expression of cognition and understanding. Empathy is an expression of feeling and caring. Use the former when the client's statement is matter of fact and the latter when it touches on something sensitive.

For example, if your client tells you a business fact about a delay in a factual manner, use *acknowledgment*: "I understand . . . has delayed . . . and your team would like another week to complete the . . . I will work with our team to explore rescheduling . . ." But if the client is upset that a key employee has resigned, which will delay the project and place additional burden on her, express *empathy*: "I am so sorry to hear Jane has resigned and this will delay . . . and set back . . . Your plate is full now, and this puts even more on you." Very often salespeople who feel empathy simply don't express it and miss the opportunity to connect with their clients.

Drill Down

Many salespeople, in their exuberance to sell, miss the chance to understand important broad or vague words their clients use. By asking questions to clarify these words you can gain tremendous insight that would be otherwise lost. For example, for the client that mentions that Jane's resignation has *implications* for the roll out, rather than assume you know what that means, ask, "I know Jane played a big role. Can you tell me more about the implications?" The implications can be timing, budget, logistics, or decision making . . . but unless you ask, you won't know.

Informed Questions

Informed questions show that you have knowledge of the client's industry, business, and/or problem. They direct the conversation to issues clients want to explore. For example, rather than ask uninformed questions, such as "Tell me what issues are of concern to you," ask informed questions like, "We see among our clients that the rate of change of protocols has been accelerating, averaging changes every four months in things such as . . . To what extent has changing protocols been an issue here?"

Rather than ask, "How is your business doing?" ask, "I noticed in . . . that you achieved a 5 percent increase in revenue this quarter. That's really great with so many other organizations in your industry struggling. We are seeing drops in . . . based on the . . . What do you attribute your superior performance to?"

> *"Be a good listener. Your ears will never get you in trouble."*
> *—Frank Tyger, editorial cartoonist*

Resolving Client Resistance

As you share insights and introduce ideas that challenge the status quo, you very likely will encounter objections. You may be thinking that there is nothing new about objections. Or is there? While objections are as old as selling itself, clients have become more risk averse and more sophisticated, which means more obstacles between you and closing at every stage of the sales process.

To resolve objections it has always been important to understand the underlying risks that concern clients. In the new environment you need not only to have the answer to the specific objection but also to be ready to support your answer with hard data or metrics and tie it back to achieving the business outcome.

Having an insight to share is especially helpful in resolving the, "I'm satisfied with my current (system [provider, process, technology])" objection. Often clients are satisfied because they aren't aware there is a better alternative and/or because they are reluctant to make a change or rock the boat. To help deal with risk aversion, the cadence of the objection model must be fortified with examples and hard data.

The traditional objection model now has two additional parts:

New Objection Resolution Model

- Acknowledge or empathize with the objection to neutralize the situation and indicate you respect the client's concerns. Use acknowledgment as a cognitive response to show you understand or empathy as a feeling response to show you care.

- Probe to narrow down what almost always will be a broad objection.

- Share knowledge that addresses the specific objection.

- *Support your position with hard data, insight, research, experience, and/or a success story.*

- *Tie your response to not only the objection but also the business outcome.*

- Check for client feedback.

Here is an example to illustrate the model.

CLIENT: I'm dependent on your three big competitors. They are important to me for training, promotions, and ideas, and they won't be happy if we do this pilot with you.

SALESPERSON: I understand that they are important in what they bring to you, and I don't want to disrupt that. You mentioned they won't be happy. What are your concerns about that?

CLIENT: Well, they will see it as a competitive threat and will remind me of all they do for me.

SALESPERSON: That's understandable, and they do bring support. I know how important it is to restore profitability to the department. What ideas have they brought to you to help restore traffic and increase profitability?

CLIENT: Nothing really. They haven't much discussed it. They say the market is tough.

SALESPERSON: The market is tough. I wanted to bring you an idea we have seen work with X client and after two months showed an increase of Y percent and an improvement in . . . I am confident that a limited pilot with specific goals will be a step in driving the traffic and profitability. This is an action we can take to give your customers an alternative and attract the ones who previously bought the expensive brands. We are projecting an increase in revenue of 8 percent, which I think is conservative. What do you think about positioning this strategy if they inquire about it as a small pilot to help restore profitability and traffic?

CLIENT: OK. Let's give it a try. It might motivate the big guys to come up with some thoughts other than coupons, and if it helps with the numbers that is exactly what I need.

Summary

If you start by recognizing that your clients are experts in their businesses, admittedly at varying levels, and that they have knowledge, perspective, and biases that you must understand to solve their problems, you will use your expertise in a way that creates collaborative conversations that lead to more sales.

To fill the business gaps your clients face, you must understand what the gaps are from their perspectives. The Create and Shape and Respond Need Models first and foremost help you plan and organize your questions to gain that knowledge and at the same time add value, guide clients' thinking, and demonstrate your focus on driving business results. At the heart of these models is Stephen Covey's fifth habit for business and personal success: "seek first to understand and then to be understood." Insight-led, informed, and insightful questions demonstrate that you know your client's world. They also help you learn what is unique about clients' worlds.

I have seen salespeople tip the scales and win major deals based on a question they asked that their competitors didn't ask. Insight-led questions turn a light bulb on in clients' heads. You are selling in the age of the client. To disrupt the status quo, you must know the status quo. If you love helping clients and if you love learning, probing with insight and knowledge provides you with a vehicle for doing both. The most effective teachers and the most effective salespeople are *expert learners* adept at teaching and learning through interaction, not lecture. Moreover, the right questions, some insight-led and some more traditional, are as powerful as the right answers and sometimes more so.

With insightful probing you set a vision and capture a picture of the world your client sees. Armed with expertise and in-depth client knowledge, you will develop solutions that bring value to your clients and sales success to you. Client knowledge, not product knowledge, differentiates. Now let's focus on creating winning solutions.

4

Value-Tracking: Shaping Solutions

"Don't just customize your solutions, personalize them."

Being able to convince a client of the superiority of a product used to be the key to sales success. For the past four decades salespeople won business based on their ability to persuade clients that their customized product solutions were better than those of their competitors. The superior product solution combined with a good relationship was the winning formula. Persuasion will always be a part of effective selling. Relationships will always be stabilizing and deeply valued. But it takes a lot more than a good product and a relationship to win business in the new sales landscape.

It is clear that what persuaded clients just a few years ago does not carry weight today. What clients value from you has changed. Your job is to know what your clients value—and to deliver it.

> *"The way to advertise is not to focus on the product."*
> —Calvin Klein

Yesterday's Value

Let's first consider what clients no longer value. Fewer and fewer clients will turn to you to learn about your products. Product as the differentiator has been marginalized. Most companies are producing quality products, and customers know they can choose from among closely matched competitors. Increased competition means not only that there are more competitors for every opportunity but also that the quality among competitors is tightly clustered, making differentiation difficult. As Neil Rackham has observed, the old business model of selling a *better* mousetrap is no longer relevant. Rather it is the consulting around things such as the appropriate traps for the site and advice on placement, bait, and safety that sells. Winning based on bigger, better, or faster is increasingly difficult because your top competitors are also selling bigger, better, faster, and often cheaper.

You can, however, differentiate your solutions through insights, ideas, advice, proof of value, and by building trusting relationships.

Changing Value

Product knowledge, of course, is a foundation, but it is a small part of what your clients value: it is the basic requirement. Clients are looking for a perspective that adds to what they know. They expect more than tailored solutions. Your goal must be to become the "go to person" who helps them anticipate issues, develop creative solutions, and achieve business and personal success.

The Product Pitch

As strange as it may seem, just a short time ago most salespeople won business by focusing on product superiority and customized fit, not impact on the business outcome (and I want to emphasize that this approach suited the times). The business outcome was addressed or implied and was the purpose of the purchase, but the business outcome was not the *core* message salespeople delivered or clients listened for. Salespeople told and sold their story based on product differentiation more than results. And while clients drove price and terms hard, the level of intensity, scrutiny, number of steps, stake-holders, and demand for proof of value was nowhere near what it is today.

Now product pitches cause frustration all around. For example, Jon was taken by surprise when his usually interested and polite client interrupted him as he was presenting his solution. His client, head of marketing, jumped in, "I can't listen to another pitch. We need to get these divisions delivering the same message and stop our president from hearing that we are confusing our customers! What can you do about that?"

Jon's message focused on his product and not on driving results. In fact Jon's solutions would deliver what his client needed to accomplish. His capabilities were right, but his conversation was wrong. He was talking customized features and benefits that described how the solution would work but missed reassurance about outcome.

Feeling the same frustration, the head of sales productivity at a major technology company said, "I disconnected my voice mail because I don't have time to listen to another product pitch." All of this points to the need for salespeople to look through a new lens as they develop and position their solutions.

> *"How you sell creates as much value as what you sell."*
> —Neil Rackham

Value Focused

The solutions that you bring to your clients are only as good as the problems they solve. Yet a recent Forrester study showed that clients believed that only *15 percent of salespeople articulate their solutions in terms of solving business problems.* This study further confirms the need for the majority of salespeople to unlearn the ingrained process of pitching product superiority and instead focus on driving business outcomes.

Thales Teixeita, assistant professor at Harvard Business School, has written about the "unconscious aversion" that people today seem to have to being persuaded.

> *"Right is meaningless if it doesn't lead to a connection."*
> —Seth Godin

Ron Johnson, the designer of the Apple buying experience and Genius Bar, attributes the willingness of Apple's clients to pay a premium for its products and reward the company with their loyalty to Apple's salespeople, who "do not focus on selling but on . . . making people's lives better." If you have shopped in an Apple store, you have likely experienced the expertise and responsiveness of the Apple team. Ron Johnson underscored that the key to selling to clients today is "helping clients achieve the *outcomes* they want."

Joel Anderson, CEO of Walmart.com, also understands the importance of selling not only what but also *how* clients want to buy. He emphasizes, "We have a lot of assets, but they're only assets if we embrace the trends of the client." Walmart is doing just that in transforming its brick-and-mortar stores into extensions of its online operations to combat showrooming (i.e., the practice of buyers trying out products in stores and then buying them online) in order to match how its clients want to buy.

While you can *influence* what clients value, at the end of the day it is clients who define value. Unless your solutions track with what they value, you won't succeed.

Client Scorecards

Clients use scorecards—some formal, some informal—as they make buying decisions. Your job is to not only know what is on each stakeholder's list but also shape it.

Although the stakeholders who make purchasing decisions generally share common goals, they have different priorities based on their roles and personal drivers. And although every client's decision-making criteria are different (it is true: God is in the details), the saving grace is that there are common criteria that appear on most clients' scorecards as they evaluate their options and make their decisions.

In working with clients across industries and product lines over the past two years, I have found that clients are focusing hard on the following points:

A Clear Connection Between Your Solution and the Desired Business Outcome

Drive home how your solution drives to the business outcome. When you focus on solving business problems during presentations you energize your clients. But when you hammer away at product features and benefits without a direct connection to solving the business issue you drain the energy in the room. The difference between talking about the product and focusing on business outcomes is startling, not subtle. One sales leader tells his team members, whether they are introducing an idea or recommending a solution, "Use industrial strength adhesive to tie what we do to achieving what the client wants to do."

In your own situation think about LinkedIn and why you joined. Was it the underlying sophisticated technology that interested you or the access to a network of contacts to grow your business and build your business acumen? Similarly, as you present your solutions *start with* and keep coming back to achieving their business outcome. Focus on the value the client derives. Start with the outcome in mind, and make the business outcome your recurring refrain.

Be sure your solution matches the level of outcome the client is seeking. The client's budget is often a good indicator. Not all solutions are equal. One client may want the near-perfect solution, another a very good one, another a good one, and another a solution that is good enough to check the box. Many salespeople lose deals, as one sales manager explained, because they build an ocean liner for a client that needs a row boat. The key is not to build what you see as the best solution possible but to provide your best advice and build the solutions that produce the outcome the client needs based on the objectives and constraints.

Proof of Past Success

Clients are risk averse. By sharing past successes you build confidence in your ability to deliver results. A key competitive edge incumbents have is that because clients know them, they perceive doing business with them as less risky.

Stories, examples, testimonials, references, research, and data are needed to give clients the confidence to change providers and/or to make a change. Success stories are one of the most effective ways to persuade clients that you will deliver. They bring your solutions to life because they make results concrete. Clients remember stories better than technical details. Moreover, stories appeal to clients' emotional side. Jonathan Gottschall, professor and author of *The Storytelling Animal,* points out that numerical and trend graphs evoke skepticism among people and provoke listeners to think of counterexamples while stories "soften" listeners and "make them easier to influence." This is not to suggest that graphs are not highly useful; a picture can be worth a thousand words. But graphs can be quickly forgotten. You will be more persuasive when you also personalize the numbers with a success story. Forrester data showed that *only 34 percent of salespeople consistently use success stories and examples.* Therefore, incorporating success stories is a way for you to give yourself a competitive edge.

To gain full impact from a success story, start by setting out the major business challenge. Then position the solution you provided and quantify the results. Conclude by relating the benefits to how your client would also benefit. Don't leave it up to your client to make the connection. Keep it brief.

Success stories can be specific to your client's industry or from a different industry as long as you make the connection clear. For example, Emily landed her company's first national retail chain by using a success story from the banking industry. She made the connection between the retail chain's new strategy to attract upscale clients and her company's deep experience and success with wealth management divisions of several major financial institutions. She showed how one client advanced from number five in market share to number two in one year. By linking the target audiences and sharing the impressive metrics she won her company's first major retail relationship.

Dylan won three new relationships based on one success story in which his call center client did not lose a single inbound call during a Super Bowl and exceeded its revenue goal. The cache of the Super Bowl relationship combined with the exceptional performance during halftime gave his clients the confidence to move ahead with the purchase.

If your organization is not making success stories available and easy to access, ask your manager to lobby marketing to create a centralized source. Do your part by benchmarking and religiously following up with your clients during and after implementation to assess results, document measurable outcomes, and add to your organization's library of success stories. Gain agreement from your clients to serve as references.

In addition to success stories use *examples, references, testimonials,* and *endorsements* to instill client confidence, add to your credibility, and help clients say yes. Almost nothing you can say will have as much influence on how your clients perceive you as an endorsement by a third party they trust. Carefully vet references and prepare them to address what your buyer cares about. For one client it may be economic impact, for others speed of delivery, responding to a competitive threat, ease of working with you and your organization, or seamless implementation.

Research, Data, and Analytics

To validate your solution, support it with data. The Aunt Jemima brand is a case in point of how research can change a client's thinking and mobilize action. For years the company's president resisted his consultant's recommendation to create pancake syrup as a part of its product line. Out of frustration the consultant included a multiple-choice question in a survey the company sponsored. He asked respondents to identify their preferred brand of pancake syrup. Of the four choices he listed, respondents selected Aunt Jemima, the only one of the four that didn't actually produce syrup, by an overwhelming majority as the number one choice. Once the consultant presented the data to the CEO along with revenue projections, the CEO made an immediate decision to start producing the syrup. Today it continues to be the leading brand in the market. The consultant looked for what wasn't there, backed up his recommendation with hard data, and created a win-win all around.

Proof of Value

Unless you move the conversation to value, you will find yourself selling on price. Value is what you have to sell as your differentiation. As clients listen to your solution they are trying to decide if it is worth the money, business and personal risk, time, energy, and attention. Bill emphasizes with his sales team, "Find something to count! Quantify what you do better and communicate what it means to each stakeholder."

Create a business case that shows economic impact by comparing the cost of the status quo and ongoing costs with the value gained through your solution. In your message and material draw a clear picture of the before and after including the cost of doing nothing. Clients are interested in return on investment (ROI), and you must show metrics. Show how your solution mitigates the risks your clients are most concerned about. For example, if adoption of the new client management system is your client's concern, position how your multiple-stage communication plan and visibility of early wins has worked in other companies. Translate that into economic impact.

Keep in mind that the value you bring will rarely be only one thing; rather, it will be a combination of the multiple elements that appear on your client's scorecard.

You know your clients want to make money, save money, and/or manage risk. But what does this look like to them? Is it improving profitability; increasing revenue; improving efficiency; achieving earnings before interest, taxes, depreciation, and amortization (EBITDA); increasing gross profit; managing cash flow; reducing operating costs; making the quarter; raising client satisfaction scores; building the brand; restoring a tarnished reputation; and so on?

Clients' roles can give you insight into what they value. For example, a CEO preparing to sell a company focuses on EBITDA, the chief technology officer (CTO) on disaster-recovery strategies, the research and development (R&D) manager on getting new products to market more quickly, the procurement officer on reducing cost and diversifying or consolidating suppliers, and the operations manager on eliminating duplication. Needs such as these are general and give you a head start in understanding a client's mindset. But you must get much more specific. Early in the sale Ellen uncovered that the procurement officer would become involved later in the process. While she could not arrange to meet with him earlier to understand his needs, she learned from her contact that he followed a strict "minimum 10 percent reduction in price and whatever else he could get to transfer risk to the seller." She used this information to develop her pricing and negotiation strategy to protect her profitability and let procurement win something too.

Insights, Ideas, and Innovation

Clients value innovation, new ideas, and insights. But what that means is often misunderstood. Innovation has become a buzzword across industries, including sales. According to M. Berkun, an innovation consultant, companies use the term to show they are on the cutting edge, agile, and cool. The *New York Times* reported that 250 books published in the past three years have the word *innovation* in the title. Many companies have chief innovation officers. Innovation is a hot topic in business schools, with 28 percent using the word *innovation* in their mission statements—usually to describe their curricula.

The problem is that real innovation or truly new product ideas—in the sense of something that never existed before—is rare. But the brilliant Mervin Kelly, architect of Bell Labs' hive of innovation, defined innovation as "a product or process that can do something better or cheaper or both" and reminded us that innovation doesn't have to be something big or that never existed before. An innovation can even be a tweak.

Fortunately, innovation comes in many varieties. Moreover, never-existed-before ideas are usually radical, nonlinear, and game-changing. By being so they are also untested and come with a higher degree of risk and can be more difficult to sell to clients who are not on the cutting/bleeding edge.

Even the genius Steve Jobs's greatest contributions weren't necessarily in innovation. As Lev Grossman, *Time* magazine's lead technology writer and book critic pointed out, Steve Jobs did not invent the iPad: "He refined and perfected it. And that was powerful, as powerful and important as the new idea itself." The key is to go from idea to impact to a winning solution. Solutions, new or old, that produce better outcomes and prove value sell.

There are many ways to innovate:

- The same solution or result but at a lower cost, for example with automation

- An idea or solution you appropriate from another client or industry

- An improvement of or customizing one feature of a product

- Simplifying a complex process, for example a universal remote

- A new product benefit that a client discovers

To know what innovations will matter to your clients, visit social media sites to understand what questions your clients are trying to answer or problems they are trying to solve. Tap into your marketing team for research and client analytics. Leverage sales tools and review research summaries.

Also look to your organization and your team to leverage its experience and thought leadership. But it takes even more. It takes being genuinely involved with your clients, having a curious nature, wanting to solve client problems, and giving yourself reflection time to be creative. You and your organization must be willing, as Steve Shapiro advised in his book *Best Practices Are Stupid*, to go beyond thinking outside the box to finding a new box. By observing your clients you can find ways to innovate and provide value. For example, Nick's acute observation and concern for his client helped him expand a small account into his largest relationship. He made his client aware of a minor opportunity to save money. The client's team members were placing multiple small orders each day and receiving multiple shipments. Nick calculated the cost, compared it to an end-of-day consolidated order and shipment, and showed a savings of $1,800 each week. While the savings was not significant, it supported his client's corporate goal to trim departmental expenses. The idea didn't initially produce revenue for Nick, but his client looked at him in a new light; within two quarters Nick was replacing his competitor. Soon his client and he were coaching each other.

In another situation, Nick helped his client use his company's latest analytic software to analyze demand data. With the analytics the client was able to tighten its marketing segmentation and messaging, cut marketing costs by 43 percent, and take steps that led to an ROI of 440 percent. He earned trusted advisor status and developed a success story that helped him win other clients.

Look at your clients and look at what is around you. Recognize what is there and what is not there. Tap into every resource. Talk with team members, colleagues, and clients to help you anticipate client needs. Think about how you can put things together or take them apart. Bring new or retreaded ideas to clients that you think can help them grow their businesses. Bring educated hunches and well-formed insights to clients. Even if they prove wrong, you have created a platform to explore why, why not, and what is relevant.

Your organization can encourage or squelch innovation. If you have freedom to question the status quo in your own organization, you will more naturally question the status quo in your clients' organizations. Opportunities to innovate are lost when knowledge, ideas, and success stories remain buried in the heads of team members or siloed in departments.

Trust

Trust is at the heart of all good relationships. Clients demand business solutions and proof of value, but if they don't trust you they won't buy from you. Even though a challenging economy and what seems like a limitless number of alternatives have made it easier for clients to count less on relationships, clients *will choose* providers they trust when other factors are relatively equal. Value may trump the relationship, but value and trust trump everything.

Trust is built during good times and bad. Trust is solidified *after* the deal when you deliver on your promise. Don't be a fair-weather friend. Maintain contact when there is no deal on the table to send the message your clients are not just transactions to you. For example, Michael Grimes, managing director of Morgan Stanley, used his computer science background and love of technology and gadgets to stay connected with his clients even when business dried up and other bankers retrenched. His visits and networking paid off when the market opened. His firm led nearly every big initial public offering including LinkedIn, Zynga, Groupon, Yandex, and Facebook.

An executive responsible for major purchases underscored the importance of trust when he said, "If I have a need, I go to colleagues and advisors I trust and ask for some names." Trust takes more than black-and-white data and metrics. It is built person to person, conversation to conversation through competency, collaboration, and open and honest dialogue.

You

You are the differentiator. You represent your organization, its culture, and its values. It is your advice and consulting, perspective, and ideas that your clients are buying. For example, if you are selling software to a health care business and the client knows you have an understanding of the legislative, economic, administrative, patient, and internal political issues they are facing, they likely will place a high value on the perspective and advice you offer.

Clients want you to be persistent and committed to helping them drive results. They want respect, but they don't want a "yes man." For example, Steve earned advisor status with his largest client because he was unrelenting in saving the client from purchasing the new crop of junk bonds that soon lived up to their name. Initially his client was emphatic about his committee's decision to buy the bonds and made it clear he did not want a counterpitch. But Steve persisted in a strong but noncontentious way. He requested a hearing with the committee and shared detailed and substantive data that showed how several respected analysts had changed their buy recommendations in the past few weeks because of a recent decline in credit quality. He leverage his depth of experience and his gut feeling along with the data. He objectively offered the pros and cons of an alternative to the bonds. He stepped out of a sales role and into an advisor role in the eyes of the client. His experience, research-based data, relationship, and belief in his message enabled him to save the client from making a costly mistake.

Forrester research showed that the sales experience is the number one factor in a client's decision to buy. So what exactly does "the sales experience" mean? Many things make up the sales experience, but clearly *you* and the conversations you lead with your clients won't have a reason to buy from you.

Know Your Value

Many salespeople stumble when it comes to talking about their value. If you can't answer *why* your clients should choose you over your competitors and do so in a clear and compelling way, they aren't likely to buy from you.

Some organizations recognize that their salespeople need help in telling their story, and they provide them with knowledge sharing and value messaging. Ideally, your sales organizations does so. Unfortunately, many sales organizations leave that up to salespeople to figure out. When that is the case you can work with your team to articulate the value you bring:

■ Bring a diverse team together: Gain perspectives from team members in sales, service, operations, marketing, training, and finance to create synergy and spark a fresher understanding.

■ Define the value your product brings to the table: Discuss value to clients in general terms to understand why they would buy the product. Once that is clear turn the focus to your product and identify what differentiates you. Keep the focus on the client and the business outcome(s) your product produces, such as growing revenue, increasing profitability, reaching new markets, changing image—and not the features and benefits of the product. Identify four to six differentiators that deliver the value to clients.

■ Test your list hard: Identify the two or three elements that truly differentiate you from your competitors. Most likely you will have to push hard to find true points of differentiation.

■ Quantifying the impact: Find a way to measure the impact your product makes with hard numbers.

Creating a Value Map

Once you understand your client's needs and have articulated the value you bring, you have the knowledge you need to construct a value map. A value map gives you a way to visualize and match the value of your offering with the outcome important to each stakeholder. In the complex sale consensus is needed, and there can be 20 or more stakeholders and multiple priorities. Creating a visual representation will help ensure the you cover all the important bases. CSO Insights reported that 40 percent of salespeople fail to identify all of the key stakeholders. This can be especially problematic if you miss addressing the priority of key players such as the executive who will make or sway the decision or a powerful influencer or adversary.

To develop a value map, create several buckets:

■ Stakeholders and roles: List the *stakeholders' names* and their *roles* (economic decision makers, influencers, users, coaches, third parties; in addition, identify supporters, naysayers, neutrals, and unknowns). For example, in a sale there may be an executive sponsor who is head of technology, an operations manager who is the direct buyer, a project manager who wants to be sure you can execute and make him or her look good, and so on. As you work with the stakeholders, be sure to identify who has the power.

- Business challenges: Identify the *business challenge* each key stakeholder is trying to solve. For example, the CFO's goal may be to consolidate providers to gain economies of scale, and the executive's focus may be to build an infrastructure that accommodates an aggressive five-year acquisition strategy.

- Business outcome: Define the *impact* each client wants to see happen.

- Proof of success: Support your solution with *proof* (e.g., research-based data and/or metrics, a success story, experience). For example, share data such as "90 percent of sales managers selected from the pool of top performers fail within two years. However, there is a 65 percent success rate when our diagnostic selection instrument is used as a part of the process. With . . . client we saw an 84 percent increase in . . . and a 75 percent reduction in turnover. In your situation . . ."

- Proof of value and reducing client risk: Clients measure value by comparing cost with the investment. Quantify the gains to the client by showing the impact of your solution on delivering the business outcome important to your client. Calculate current and future costs to show your client the benefits of making a change. Present financial and nonfinancial impact. For example, show the cost of turnover in dollars and/or damage control.

■ Other priorities: Align your solution to all other criteria important to your client whether that is innovation, culture, brand recognition, or a promotion.

A value map will help you organize and customize the elements of your solution to each key stakeholder and make your case for change. For example, if the senior vice president of sales is focused on reducing sales force turnover and improving forecasting accuracy, your solution must show how your profiling tool reduces sales force turnover by X percent and how your sales manager playbook will improve forecasting and results by Y percent.

Structure Your Solution

Business problems are complex and the solutions can be equally complex. Your job is to present solutions in the simplest terms while conveying the full value you deliver. Siegel and Etzkora, in their book *Simple*, pointed out that "more information is not more clarity." The content of your solution is the end product of your research, conversations with your clients and team members, experience, observations, brainstorming, and creative thinking. Once you answer the questions, "What does the client really want to accomplish?" and "What does this client value?" the next task is to organize your value message so it's easy for your clients to understand and say yes to. *How* you tell your story is as important as the story itself in shaping your client's perception of your value. By having a structure to follow you can organize your content from your value map

> "You have to work hard to get your thinking clean. But it's worth it because in the end once you get there you can move mountains."
> —Steve Jobs

more easily and persuasively. One of the best things about structure is that in and of itself it is persuasive because it gives the impression of thoughtful and organized mind.

The Value Solution Model

Use the Value Solution Model to help you pull together all the threads of the message from your value map. Structure your solution so that it is clear, focused on solving the business problem, and compelling. Connect every element to the business outcome.

> *". . . simplify, simplify . . . the necessary and the real . . ."*
> —Henry David Thoreau

Timothy Cook, Apple's CEO, captured the importance of this when he said, "I am not sure how many megahertz my iPod operates on . . . or the technology inside the technology anymore. I just know it works." Moving from product to outcome for most salespeople will take an overhaul, not a tweak.

The value you bring will rarely be one thing. *It is the combination, not a single point of your solution*, that creates differentiation. Using the Value Solution Model will help you organize all the parts of your story so that it moves clients to act.

Value Solution Model

Position the Business Challenge

■ Acknowledge the challenge and the importance of the outcome.

Support with Insight and Data

■ Make the bottom-line impact the first and recurring message.

Position Your Customized Solution (tie elements of solution to business outcome)

- Provide a high-level overview of solution.

- Position the solution.

- Show how technical elements to solve the business challenge and tie to outcome.

- Support with research.

- Show proof of success/success story and check for questions.

- Prove value with hard metrics, and ROI to show financial impact. Make a comparison with current and ongoing costs, and check for questions.

Position Team and Show Ease of Implementation

- Review team members' roles and expertise.

- Share realistic time frames that meet client needs, and check for questions and/or objections.

- Express competence and commitment to partner with client and check for questions.

Check for Client Agreement

- Ask how solution achieves business outcome.

- Ask for the business or next step.

The Value Solution Model at Work

Jon was vigilant in keeping current on the industries he worked with. He was aware that sales of beauty products were down again this month in all big box stores. He had a relationship with a highly sophisticated big box store that had been hit particularly hard by the recession. The manager of the health and beauty department was under severe pressure to increase store traffic and restore profitability to his department. Business was down 21 percent. Although the manager had mounds of big data, client analytics, and 10 years of experience, he had not been able to increase traffic or restore profitability.

Jon brought up his client's challenge with his team during a bimonthly phone sales meeting. He explained that the department offered two tiers of beauty products: the expensive salon brands and the discounted brands. One of the salespeople shared a strategy in which her retail clothing client created a mid-priced "designer-inspired" department as a third alternative that sat between the expensive and discounted brands to attract clients and increase the amount of the average sale. Jon recognized that this could work for his client and saw this as a chance to grow this high-potential relationship.

He set a meeting with the manager, recapped the challenge, shared data about the impact the economy was having on clients' buying habits of "luxury" products by either stopping clients from buying health and beauty products altogether or causing them to switch to the less expensive discounted brands. He asked for his client's perspective.

He positioned his idea for a three-tier strategy by setting up a mid-priced product display between the expensive salon brands and discounted product sections. He described the retail chain's success story, compared the current approach with the new approach, and projected revenue targets for financial impact. He offered SalonInspired as a catchy name for the new section and offered to set up the display at no cost to the store, reinforcing the ease of working with him.

When he checked for the manager's reaction, he was able to resolve his objection about the problem this could cause for his client with the three big suppliers the client relied on heavily for displays, training, and product promotions. Jon resolved the objection by proving what ideas they had brought to help increase sales or restore store traffic and reinforced his confidence that this would increase traffic and profitability. When the department manager raised the issue of how this would look to his district manager if the strategy didn't work, Jon offered to assume full accountability and share the idea with her. By keeping the focus on business outcome and reviewing financial projections, Jon landed a six-week pilot.

Jon's relationship-management skills paid off too. Several months earlier when he was on vacation in Europe he had e-mailed photos of unique store displays to his contact and the district manager he had met once very briefly. By leveraging this one contact with her, Jon arranged a short phone conversation in which he described the pilot, assumed full responsibility, and gained her support.

By the fifth week the pilot exceeded its goal. Initially the pilot was extended, but after three months Jon got the go-ahead for a national rollout. That mid-priced salon product section is now a staple throughout all locations.

Jon did all the right things to *create value* for his client, his organization, and himself. He developed an expertise in his niche and shared insights with an educated client whom he was committed to helping. He leveraged his team to help solve a client's problem. He repositioned his beauty product line, which at one time had been sold in salons, as the mid-priced option between the expensive and discounted brands. He differentiated not by focusing on the features and benefits and why his product line was better than his big competitors' but by *focusing on solving the business problem*. In fact, he barely discussed the features and benefits of his line. He worked backward into his offering from his focus on driving business results. Yes, he had a very good product. His product had always been good. But his consulting, sharing of insights, and idea (not his product), won the day. He came to the table as an equal and left as a thought partner. His client learned from him as a partner, not a student, and Jon developed a success story to help him win his next deal.

Delivery Advantage

How you deliver insights, ideas, and solutions affects how your clients think about them. A study by Marie-Line Germain and Manuel Tejeda in the summer 2012 *HRD Quarterly* pointed to the importance of subjective factors such as self-assurance and confidence in whether clients see a presenter as an expert. To gain the advantage of a confident delivery, *practice* and *ask for feedback* not only on your strategy, content, and structure but also on your delivery (e.g., demeanor, pacing, style, tone, dress, and body language). And this is especially important when you are delivering new or provocative ideas or selling high-ticket, high-visibility solutions.

Clients want to hear and see what *you* bring to the table. They are not impressed by a prepackaged set of slides. Don't use a deep stack of PowerPoint slides, especially in a dark room. Of course, well-developed and edited slides and technology can enhance presentations, but you, not they, are the presentation. Your clients must feel your recommendation comes from you and not a screen. Slide presentations often communicate *to* clients. To win, communicate *with* clients.

If you could magically peek in on a competitor's presentation, how would you compare? Would you come across as professional, confident, and ready to stand shoulder to shoulder with the client to get the job done? While you can't see your competitors' presentations and make comparisons, your clients can and are doing precisely that as they make their decisions.

As you practice, pay particular attention to the pace and emphasis of your words. Separate your language. Move with a sense of direction. The best teacher captures the class not only with good, clear content but also with intonation, pacing, and movement. A senior executive wondered why the presentation he worked very hard on was received so poorly by his audience of corporate leaders. A review of the videotape of his presentation provided the answer: the content was strong and current yet all but impossible to follow. There was no emphasis or pausing, and his arms seemed almost as if they were flapping.

Use your voice to drive home key points and emphasize what is important. *There should be a beat to how you present.* Pauses show you want clients to absorb what you have said. Two seconds of silence before answering a question shows you are considering the question. Your gestures orchestrate how your clients should listen. Use them to accentuate and delineate the points you make.

Summary

In a complex sale the dialogue takes place over a series of meetings with multiple stakeholders. In each conversation your job is to demonstrate that you can add value. All your work culminates when you present your solution. Winning solutions solve business problems and quantify value.

When you make your recommendations, the stakes are high. Use the value map to configure a solution that incorporates all of the crucial decision-making criteria that the stakeholders are assessing. Value is what your clients buy and what you must deliver. Let's now focus on creating a shared sales and buying process to help ensure you understand and influence what your clients value and move them to buy more quickly from you.

5

Phasing: Controlling
the Process

"The traditional sales process is a thing of the past."

A sales process maps out the stages of a sale. Until recently it was the sales process, whether formal or random, that drove the sale. But today it is the client's buying process that drives the sale. In the old days—just a few years ago—salespeople found clients, qualified opportunities, probed needs, and communicated customized product knowledge. Now clients at all levels use searches to find alternatives, self-educate, and narrow down the providers *they choose to contact.* Their buying habits have created an entirely new sales landscape. As a result salespeople face a new set of sales obstacles and opportunities.

This shift in control from seller to buyer demands a reengineering of how you sell. Many clients have carefully defined their buying process. They calculate their purchases. For example, procurement has become a late-in-the-sale opportunity for buyers to get a second bite at the apple and eat into your profits. Many clients know the ropes because they have done their homework or have made the same or a similar purchase before. But there are also clients, particularly first-time buyers who learn as they go, who are unaware of alternatives to improve their situation. Opportunity to add value exists, whether clients are knowledgeable or novice or whether they are significantly through their buying cycle or just beginning. Where you enter a client's buying cycle is, nevertheless, a big factor in how much influence you have. If you fall behind or run ahead, they won't wait or try to catch up.

> *". . . when an effective sales process is in place, win rates move from 42 percent to 52 percent."*—CSO Insights

Client's Buying Process

Once clients have set their business goals and objectives and identified the obstacles that stand in the way of success, they identify strategies and initiatives to remove the obstacles. This means change and frequently sets them on a search for information and solutions. As a part of that search clients go through buying stages. Understanding these stages and the activities within each stage helps you to align with and influence how, when, and what your clients buy. In general there are six buying stages:

Stage 1: Awareness

In stage 1 clients recognize an obstacle (e.g., management, competitors, operations, products, market, financial) that is blocking them from achieving their goals and objectives. They evaluate how important each obstacle is to identify the priorities. Some of the problems are longstanding, and others catch them by surprise, but they focus on the priorities that require immediate attention.

When clients don't recognize that they are facing a challenge or missing an opportunity, you have the opportunity to create awareness and disrupt their satisfaction with the status quo. By bringing an insight or idea before clients in stage 1, you jump-start their buying cycle and create a competitive advantage in the influence you have over the buying outcome.

Stage 2: Options

In stage 2 clients research the alternatives available to them. They analyze their options, consider their ability to solve the problems themselves, and begin to weigh the politics and costs.

They identify possible internal and external providers. They compare approaches and define their decision criteria. They further consider the importance and cost of staying with the status quo and begin to build a case for change.

Stage 3: Research and Comparison of Solutions

In stage 3 clients narrow down the shortlist of providers they will contact and consider; refine requirements and criteria; and think through the financial, personal, and political risks to making a change. They continue to refine decision criteria, issue a request for information (RFI) or request for proposals (RFPs), or directly contact and meet with providers to assess capabilities, resolve concerns, assess fit, and continue to evaluate the purchase against other priorities.

Stage 4: Selection, Negotiation, and Contract

In stage 4 clients schedule presentations and demonstrations with providers on their short lists, weigh the risk and reward of each competitor's solution, achieve consensus, make a final decision, negotiate the contract, secure final approval and signatures, and prepare to execute.

Stage 5: Execution

In stage 5 clients identify their implementation team and, as appropriate, lead a change initiative. During the implementation they evaluate the experience and ease of working with you, your team, and your organization against the sales promise and commitment you made to them.

Stage 6: Business Outcome

In stage 6 clients evaluate results and the business impact against the metrics they established at the outset. They get formal and informal feedback from stakeholders to assess how well the results justified the cost. They decide whether they want to continue or expand their relationship with you.

The six stages of the buying cycle provide a general framework. To gain real leverage fill in specific details for each of your clients. Understanding the *details* of your client's buying process pays off. Nancy was working feverishly to close a $275,000 deal for the third quarter. In her second meeting with her client (two months before she won the deal) she elicited numerous details about the client's buying process and learned that once her client completed a purchase order it would be reviewed by legal and sent to procurement. After that the contract would be signed by a manager in Brazil using an electronic signature. She requested the e-mail addresses and cell phone numbers of all the parties, and with her client's OK she introduced herself by e-mail to the international contacts. Her intimate knowledge of her client's process coupled with her excellent deal-management skills enabled her to reach the manager in Brazil by phone and get him to sign the contract electronically on Saturday, July 31, at 6:15 p.m.—just before the close of her third quarter. She had her team on call so the system could go live and the revenue could be recognized for the quarter. She demonstrated what it takes to regain control of the sales process and win. She understood what her client needed and valued and delivered it. She understood not only why but exactly how her client would make the buying decision.

Intercept the Client's Buying Cycle

Because many clients today are moving through their buying cycle before talking with you, you can have less selling time to affect their decisions. In the past, with about 90 percent of a client's buying cycle available to you, you had time to learn, persuasively make your case, and connect. The challenge now is to find ways to create more time and intercept the buying cycle as early as possible.

In every stage of the buying cycle expectations are high, and clients require different things from you depending on the stage they are on.

If you are responding to a prequalified lead from your marketing team in which a client has requested information and contact, the client may be in stage 2. But if you learn about the opportunity through an RFP, your client is likely in late stage 3 and is much more interested in talking about achieving the business outcome.

The earlier in the cycle you engage, the better. But in every stage of the client's buying cycle you have a chance to shape the client's thinking.

Of course, you don't have total control of where you intercept a buying cycle. In your pipeline you likely have a mix of opportunities: some that you have created, some you have shaped, and others you are responding to. If you are like most salespeople, when you analyze the opportunities in your pipeline you find that your opportunities are weighted toward the respond and shape modes. By relying on the respond mode, rather than proactively generating ideas and creating opportunities, you will find yourself in competitive and price-driven sales. The later you enter the buying cycle, the more challenging it is to influence the decision criteria, differentiate your solution, and get paid for value. With the data available to you today, you (ideally supported by your marketing team) can gain visibility into clients that allows you to anticipate their needs and bring insights and ideas to them early in the process.

Win–Loss Reviews

The postsale period is an incredibly valuable time to learn about how your clients buy. Win–loss reviews are one of the best ways to gain insights into purchase decisions—and how you performed. Even though at this point it is too late to change the outcome of a lost deal, in my experience there is almost nothing as illuminating as a win–loss review. Win–loss reviews provide insights that help you win more business by:

■ Identifying and correcting gaps in your sales process

■ Recognizing trends

■ Learning where you, your team, and your solutions need help

■ Identifying your strengths

■ Illuminating areas for coaching

■ Gaining a deeper understanding of the client's buying process

■ Learning about competitors

■ Discovering client benefits not anticipated

Debrief *all* deals, win or lose. Aberdeen research showed that best-in-class sales organizations are 25 percent more likely to deploy formal win–loss analysis around opportunities. Laggard companies (i.e., the poorest performing) are 50 percent more likely *not* to conduct win–loss reviews.

Without a doubt, once you get a decision you ask your client for feedback. However, these discussions, based on my experience, produce little insight. If you have won you are too elated, and if you lose you and your client are not usually in a state of mind to go into depth. In addition, clients are more forthcoming in providing candid feedback to a third party. Therefore, once you complete your postsale debrief with your client, if you really want to know the score ask a third party such as your manager or a trusted colleague who was *not* directly involved in the sale to conduct a formal win–loss review with your clients.

Many salespeople are reluctant to have deals scrutinized by a manager or colleague. It takes guts, an openness to hearing the good, the bad, and the ugly, and a desire to be the best. Having a colleague make the call may seem like a bitter pill to swallow, but it will provide you with insights into your wins and losses that will help you win more and more deals—and often your very next one. The majority of clients will be frank and view the request for formal feedback as a positive sign of your organization's professionalism and your commitment for ongoing improvement.

In order to avoid tainting the feedback, don't alert your client that your colleague will be making contact. When you ask your colleague to set up the win–loss call, prepare him with background on the opportunity and a copy of a win–loss review guide that will help him get as much specific feedback as possible (see Win–Loss tool in Appendix).

> *"Sixty percent of opportunities in the pipeline result in no decision."*
> —Brainshark

Your Sales Process

Closing rates are down, the number of no decisions are up, and the Aberdeen Group has reported that sales forecasting accuracy averages about 50 percent (77 percent for best-in-class sales organizations, 69 percent for average organizations, and a low of 31 percent for lagging organizations). Moving deals through the pipeline is on every sales leader's and salesperson's mind.

Companies that follow a defined sales process are more likely to move opportunities through their pipelines more quickly, forecast more accurately, and close more deals. An effective sales process is very specific, defining:

■ The major *stages* in the sales cycle

■ *Objectives* to accomplish in each stage

- *Selling activities* to carry out in each stage based on *best practices* of top performers and research

- *Verifiable outcomes* to spell out *actions that clients must take* to signal their readiness (and therefore your readiness) to move to the next stage so you can realistically assess the opportunity

- *Sales tools* to support your sales efforts in each stage

- *Dialogue models* to help you deliver your message clearly and persuasively

By aligning your sales process with your client's buying cycle, you make better decisions. You help clients make better decisions. You do the right things at the right time with the right clients and team members.

Steps in the Sales Process

Most sales processes follow a similar sequence. The following sales process covers six fundamental stages and can be used as a guide to refine, change, or develop the sales process that is right for you:

Stage 1: Target and Qualify

Objectives

- Identify your most productive sources of leads.

- Target clients that meet your ideal client profile and qualify them.

- Gain referrals and leverage social networking.

- Contact clients and gain agreement to move to the next step.

Best Practices Activities

- Research industry, company, and stakeholders.

- Develop a relevant insight to share—a value message.

- Prepare qualifying and business challenge questions.

- Enter data in customer relationship management (CRM) software.

Verifiable Outcomes

- Engage with qualified client, gauge interest, and schedule meeting.

Sales Tools

- LinkedIn (see Chapter 2)

- Sales meeting planner

- CRM

Self- and Sales Manager Coaching Questions

- Why does this client qualify?

- At what stage am I entering the client's buying cycle?

- Am I selling in a create, shape, or respond mode?

- What is my level of up-to-date industry knowledge?

- What insight will I share to add value and engage?

- What are the business challenges driving the solution I feel can be meaningful to this client?

- Who in the client's organization cares about this challenge?

Dialogue Model

- Insight Model (Insight Statement Template)

In stage 1 you identify prospects who meet your ideal client profile or you cross-sell into a current relationship to create or respond to an opportunity. By 2014 it is predicted that up to 80 percent of clients will find you before you find them. When clients contact you they have done some level of homework, and you must understand the steps they have taken up to that point and learn what their next steps will be. For clients who contact you through the Internet, review data from your marketing group to understand their web thumbprint. Gauge their interest based on the number of visits, time spent, and areas of focus, and use that information to prepare a relevant insight.

Stage 2: Explore and Assess

Objectives

- Identify the business challenge, potential opportunity.

- Identify and arrange to meet the executive sponsor and other stakeholders.

- Prepare and review validation e-mail and gain client feedback.

Best Practices Activities

- Confirm that the client qualifies.

- Share your prepared insight.

- Explore the business challenge and opportunity.

- Identify decision makers and rank client decision criteria.

- Engage with multiple stakeholders.

- Position the high level of your approach or idea.

- Identify and cultivate a client coach(es) who will advocate for you.

- Identify a client(s) to coach.

- Map needs, politics, decision criteria, and metrics to stakeholders.

- Develop and send validation e-mail that summarizes your understanding of the client's needs and desired outcome.

- Update CRM.

Verifiable Outcomes

- Identify and access stakeholders, including executives.

- Gain feedback on validation e-mail.

Sales Tools

- Sales call planner

- Value map

- CRM

Self- and Sales Manager Coaching Questions

- What problem is the client trying to solve?

- What outcome does the client want to achieve?

- Where does this initiative fit with the client's corporate priorities?

- Who are the stakeholders?

- Who is the executive sponsor?

- What level of access do I have?

- What obstacles could come up that could block moving forward?

- What is the client's buying process?

- How have I validated this? With whom?

- Is this opportunity worth pursuing?

- How do I differentiate?

During stage 2 identify and reach stakeholders, including the executive, understand what options the client is considering, learn about the decision criteria, and differentiate yourself and your organization. Expand beyond your one point of contact.

Stage 3: Access and Develop

Objectives

- Access executive(s) and leverage your team members. Begin to draft your solution based on the unique value you bring.

- Schedule final presentation.

Best Practices Activities

- Explore the risks the client is concerned about.

- Confirm the decision-making process, key stakeholders and needs, risks clients are concerned about, politics, scope, timelines, and priorities.

- Identify the competitive landscape to create your competitive strategy.

- Connect on a personal level with clients.

- Build consensus among stakeholders.

- Test the solution and gain feedback from your coach, clients, and team.

- Identify a relevant success story and calculate proof of value.

- Develop your proposal.

- Prepare your team for the presentation.

- Update CRM.

Verifiable Outcomes

- Confirm the business challenge with executive.

- Gain agreement from the client to time, participants, and expectations for your presentation.

- Develop the proposal and agenda.

- Lead practice session with your team.

Sales Tools

- Value map

- CRM

Self- and Sales Manager Coaching Questions

- How am I differentiating my solution?

- How does my solution solve the business challenge? Achieve the business outcome?

- Have I incorporated the executive's priorities into the solution?

- Does my proof of value include financial impact?

- What are the risks that concern the stakeholders? How will I mitigate the risks?

- What metrics will the client use to evaluate the solution?

- Who are the competitors?

- How do we rank among the competitors?

- What is my competitive strategy?

- What references will I use?

- How relevant is my success story?

- Who will participate in the presentation from the client's team?

- Who is needed on my team?

- When is the practice session for my team?

In stage 3 your clients are listening to and evaluating competitive presentations. The solution and proposal you develop must convince stakeholders that you will produce the outcome critical to them and that the solution has positive financial impact. Focus on how you will solve the business challenge, mitigate risks, and deliver results with hard metrics.

Stage 4: Position Solution and Follow Up

Objectives

- Deliver a customized presentation that drives business results.

- Elicit client feedback on your presentation.

Best Practices Activities

- Practice with your team.

- Debrief with your team.

- Gain feedback from your client, coach, and other clients, and maintain contact.

- Address unanswered client questions and objections, and maintain contact.

- Develop and execute a closing strategy.

- Strategize for the negotiation, and manage procurement.

- Collaborate with client on the next steps.

Verifiable Outcomes

- Debrief with team.

- Obtain client feedback on the presentation.

- Set time for final round (if there is a final round, refine your solution based on client feedback and prepare your team).

Sales Tools

- Refine value map.

- Value Solution Model.

Self- and Sales Manager Coaching Questions

- When will I debrief with my team?

- From whom will I get postpresentation client feedback?

- What questions and objections remain?

- How will I refine my solution?

- How will I follow up to maintain contact and exert influence?

In stage 4 clients assess risks versus rewards and work to gain consensus and make the decision. Maintain contact throughout the decision process to show interest and reinforce and position or reposition your value.

Stage 5: Close and Negotiate

Objectives

- Reach agreement on refined solution and scope.

- Negotiate price and terms to conclude a win–win agreement.

Best Practices Activities

- Follow up to gain feedback.

- Respond to any open issues.

- Gain and confirm commitment that client will move forward with you.

- Develop and present a contract, and get a signature.

- Conduct win–loss debrief with client.

- Debrief with your team.

Verifiable Outcomes

- Prepare for a win–win negotiation (e.g., price, terms, objective, bottom line, trades, and must haves).

- Reach verbal agreement.

- Obtain purchase order.

- Sign contract.

- Update CRM.

Sales Tools

- Electronic signature

- Win–loss tool

Self- and Sales Manager Coaching Questions

- What client questions and issues remain open?

- What is my closing strategy?

- How am I instilling a sense of urgency?

- What are the client's expectations in regard to actions, timeline, and challenges?

- When and to whom was the contract presented?

- What was the feedback?

- Where are we in the steps to get the contract signed?

- With whom will I negotiate?

- What are the essentials and trades for my negotiation?

- What is my objective and bottom line?

- What negotiation insights have I gotten from my coach?

- What are the next steps?

In stage 5 clients check references if they have not already done so, secure final approval to move forward, and make their decision. Follow up, gain feedback, answer questions, execute a well-planned closing strategy, negotiate the contract, and promptly get a signature. Debrief the sale with your client and team.

Stage 6: Implement, Maintain, and Expand

Objectives

- Transition to implementation team for successful execution.

- Gain feedback from your team and client.

- Introduce other resources and offerings to expand and strengthen the relationship.

Best Practices Activities

- Arrange with a team member not directly involved in the sale to conduct the win–loss review. (Please see Win–Loss tool in Appendix.)

- Share win–loss feedback with team.

- For wins, ask your executive to place a thank you call to the client (for some losses this is merited, especially if you were the incumbent).

- Seek client feedback throughout and post implementation.

- Seek feedback from your team.

- Maximize results with formal status reports to client to reinforce your value. If there are problems, acknowledge and work to resolve them.

- Develop and share your team's success story within your organization.

- Create a strategy to expand the current relationship and across divisions.

- Ask for referrals.

Verifiable Outcomes

- Gain client feedback.

- Conduct win–loss review.

- Identify next opportunity.

Sales Tools

- Win–loss review tool (see Appendix)

Self- and Sales Manager Coaching Questions

- What did I learn from the debrief with my team?

- Who will conduct my win–loss review?

- What have I learned individually, for the team, and for my organization?

- How will I share the client feedback?

- What feedback have I gotten from my client about the implementation and our team?

- How can I support my client and my team?

- How well did the initiative deliver the business outcome?

- What are the metrics?

- Did the solution justify the cost?

- In which areas of the company do I think there is opportunity to expand?

- Who can I leverage to grow the relationship?

- What is my next step?

- How can I share knowledge and insights with this client and my team on an ongoing basis?

- Can I get a client testimonial?

In stage 6 your sale is far from over. In fact, it is just the beginning. Your role varies based on your company's structure. It can range from immediate transition from you to your team or full execution by you. If you transition to your team, prepare team members and follow up with them.

Your clients are evaluating the purchase against their expectations and the experience of working with your organization. To make that experience as positive as possible, continue to get feedback from your clients and your team.

Follow-up can be challenging, especially for hunters. Data from Chally and Caliber showed that when hunters are left responsible for a relationship, the life of the relationship rarely exceeds three years. It is disheartening to know that clients begin to look to change providers after 27 months and that the attrition of present relationships for most companies is 15 to 20 percent each year. Paying attention post sale is one important way to reduce attrition. Ideally your sales organization is freeing you up with sales tools and a support team that allow you to spend more time on after-sales client satisfaction and growing relationships.

Best Practices, Best Bet

One of the most effective ways to increase sales performance is to build best practices into a sales process. Best practices define the behaviors and activities of top performers for each stage of the sales process and serve as a how-to for closing more business. For example, a pharmaceutical firm recognized that the majority of its sales revenue came from 30 percent of its sales force. In an effort to increase the productivity of its mid-performers, it identified two best practice activities exhibited by the 30 percent. One of the challenges faced in this business is that when a rep makes a sale to a hospital group, each group within the organization must comply before revenue is recognized. The top performers found a way to make this happen. By reviewing the best practices of the 30 percent, the sales leader observed that those reps gained compliance by consistently carrying out prescheduled follow-up meetings that they made a part of the contract. These meetings allowed them to keep an eye on the status of orders and payments and determine whether the commitment was being met. They also held monthly feedback sessions with the clients to ensure their clients were highly satisfied and used the meeting to promote compliance. The sales leader embedded these two best practices into stage 6 of the sales process as a performance standard. The result: an additional 15 percent of the sales force gained compliance within three months.

Ask yourself these questions about all the deals in your pipeline:

- Have I completed the best practices activities for each stage?

- What verifiable actions has the client taken to indicate his or her readiness to move forward to the next stage with me?

- Do I have enough deals in my pipeline to make the quarter?

- How long have these opportunities been in this stage? (If it is more than two times longer than the average time for comparable opportunities, it is likely time to make a decision about your strategy and the opportunity.)

- For large or strategically important opportunities, have I asked for coaching and team support?

- Am I leveraging all the resources that I need in order to win this opportunity?

- Who else might I involve?

You will likely engage with your clients multiple times in each stage of the process through phone calls, meetings, and mobile contact. There may be some reversals before going forward, but a well-defined sales process will help ensure you take every step you can to position yourself to win.

Summary

Best-in-class sales organizations provide their sales teams with a clearly defined sales process. Yet only a small percentage of sales organizations have a formal sales process in place. Even those that do have a process may need to reengineer it to align with the new buyer. According to McKinsey, 75 percent of sales process implementation is not adopted by the sales force. Adoption means change. Of course, it is easy to blame lack of adoption on sales leadership because much depends on their setting accountability standards and actively reinforcing the process. But it has been my experience that the sales process can live and die with midlevel sales managers. Without that any sales process can easily languish. But even without support you can take individual responsibility, and with observation,

research, and collaboration with your team, you can c(
your own sales process if one has not been provided.

The best sales process is only as good as the discipline you put
into it and the conversations you lead to execute it. It's up to you to
scout out best practices, carry out the activities, use the tools, and
tap into every resource to maximize every minute and every word
of every client conversation. Following a sales process is like exer-
cise; once you get into it, it becomes a habit. Process is the science
side of selling. Now let's look at its heart.

6

Linking: Connecting Emotionally

"You are client-centered. Are you also human-centered?"

Rose was competing for a large opportunity with an international bank. Up to that point her contact was Bill, a mid-level manager and gatekeeper. The current relationship was limited to two small projects. After reading a blog about accessing executive decision makers, Rose let her contact know that at the request of her senior vice president (SVP) she would be contacting the department executive to request a meeting. In her e-mail Rose referenced her contact's helpfulness, shared a relevant insight about process adoption, and cc'd her contact. Within two weeks she and her SVP met with Bill and the executive.

The executive, an attorney by training with an MBA and a $12 million budget, started the meeting by saying, "You've worked with us for three years. Where have you been? You have never met with me. You have never even contacted me. *I want to feel the love.* I am sure from the e-mail you have some value for us. Why haven't you been talking to me?" Not many executives are so inviting, but her choice of words—"feel the love"—was telling. In this digital era clients are bombarded with information, data, research studies, insights, and ideas. What does it take for clients to *feel the love*? All the data and insights in the world can't deliver that—but you can. At the same time you drive value, think about the values you drive and the level of trust you are building.

> *"Great drummers play not just the beat but the song."*
> —George Harrison (speaking of Ringo Starr)

You will build deeper, longer, and more profitable relationships when there is a connection based on open and honest dialogues. Every conversation you have with your clients leaves an emotional imprint. The question is, do you know what that imprint looks like?

Technology has put what seems like infinite knowledge at your and your clients' fingertips. Clients can get answers to their questions quickly on their own. Advances such as Google's autosuggest can even anticipate a question before a person completes asking it. Unprecedented access to knowledge makes it tempting to think that all you need is superior industry and client knowledge and relevant insights and ideas to succeed. With all of the cutting-edge tools and quick access to data, it is also easy to think your success hinges there. Certainly you must have knowledge and tools and bring value to your clients to compete and win—but what else?

> *"Being transparent means your heart is exposed and your head is on fire."*
> —Wendy Lea, CEO, Get Satisfaction

Expertise and tools aren't the full package. When the executive mentioned *feeling the love*, what was she talking about? Not only ideas. Not only business solutions. She was talking about the emotional part of the sales experience. As contradictory as it may seem, technology that gives us ever-increasing ways to connect has made it harder to feel connected.

We are living in a cognitive age where data helps us make sense of complex issues and provides an objective perspective to help us make better decisions. But it is a mistake to lose sight of the powerful role that emotions play in your clients' business decisions.

Sales is filled with emotions. In a recent *New York Times* op-ed article, David Brooks demonstrated how feelings, relationships, and values prevailed over hard data. He described how the CEO of a large bank continued to do business in a country and ride out a potential crisis even though his decision conflicted with the data that his team pooled together showing a downside scenario and short-term costs. The CEO was guided by a different way of thinking. David Brooks explained it: "Commerce depends on trust. Trust is reciprocity created by emotions." Every day in offices emotional reactions dislodge deeply formed logical conclusions.

As Leary, Pillemer, and Wheeler pointed out in their *HBR* article "Negotiating with Emotion," "High stake deal making is fraught with feelings. Should we really ignore that?" And Bruce Tempken, VP and principal analyst at Forrester, reinforced that selling is filled with emotion when he said, "Every interaction creates a personal reaction."

When you learn something, the learned information begins to fade unless it is reinforced. But when you have a strong emotional experience, you *never* forget it. In his book *Emotions Never Sleep*, Donald Gephart, former dean at Rowan University, explains that even though emotions never sleep, cognition does.

One of the reasons success stories are so powerful in selling, as research has shown again and again, is that stories tap into emotions and create empathy. Tolstoy was right that a story is an infection and "the infection is emotion." The words *emotions* and *trust* don't appear in requests for proposals (RFPs) or proposals. But they are as prevalent in decision making as anything in an RFP or a client's scorecard.

Selling with Heart to Build Trust Early

Trust can be earned after you have delivered the business outcome. But how can you build trust earlier in the sales process? Your clients spend a lot of time considering how they *feel* about things—just as you do. And although they are using metrics and analytics to carefully evaluate their options, their feelings about you are also busily at work from the first conversation through to the point where they make a decision. Your emotions are busy too, and you must recognize and channel them to focus on not only the opportunity but also what is happening in the relationship. Emotional reactions are strong, and you must be aware of them and take measures to manage them. Salespeople learn how to stay cool and wear a game face, but no time is spent talking about developing a warm heart. No time is spent talking about the vulnerability needed to have open and honest dialogues that register positively on clients' trust meters. Daniel Pink's book *To Sell Is Human* looks at selling from a human point of view. He understands the "heart" part of selling and gave this advice to his readers: "Make it personal and make it purposeful."

> "Everything has an emotional content and a pragmatic content."
> —David Kelly, Founder, IDEO

How much heart is in your selling? Beyond asking yourself about *what* you do, it's important to ask *how* you do it. Do you sell with the *heart of a seller (closer)*? Do you sell with the *heart of a teacher (helper)*? Can you sell with both? We all know how critical drive is to sales success. No one disputes that—and rightly so. But how important is it to sell with heart too? David Kelly, founder of IDEO (which fashioned Apple's mouse and P&G's Swiffer) feels the most important thing in business is to be human-centered. Being human-centered is quite different from being client- or customer-centered.

When you sell with heart, you don't treat clients like transactions. Of course you deliver for them, but they know you care about them. It is the combination of competence and caring that builds trust.

What is buying if it is not a gesture of trust? Trust has always been hard earned in business, but recent conditions have made clients more cynical. You are the representative of trust for your organization. When clients trust you, they open up to you, they listen to you, they partner with you, and they are more apt to buy from you. Trust makes perceived risks acceptable. But when there is no trust, soon there is no relationship. A Fortune 500 client ended a

12-year, million-dollar-plus annual contract, despite being very satisfied with the technical product and implementation team. When she called the president of the company that had been providing the service to tell him that her company was not renewing its contract, she asked the company's president, "Tell me. Isn't a million-dollar-a-year relationship big enough to warrant someone who cares?" She explained that the salesperson had gotten complacent but more importantly "didn't fit in." After some probing the president learned that in a meeting with an executive the salesperson tried to bluff her way when it was clear she wasn't prepared and didn't have the answer—a mistake that was antithetical to the client's culture. The client said, "The question wasn't important. But we need someone we can trust."

The 2012 Eldelman Trust Barometer revealed that between 2011 and 2012 trust plummeted from the previous low of 43 percent to 38 percent for CEOs and a low of 34 percent to 29 percent for government. This may not surprise you. But what may be surprising is that while academics and technical experts continued to get the highest ratings for trust, with academics at 78 percent (teachers and researchers) and technical experts at 68 percent (subject matter experts), the highest group to gain on the trust meter were regular employees, gaining 16 percent for a total of 66 percent.

> *"Emotion isn't going to go away. . . . Instead it is going to influence the story we tell ourselves."*
> —Seth Godin

Statistics such as this reinforce how key your role is. They point to the need to demonstrate expertise and approach clients with as much a teacher hat as a sales hat if you want clients to trust your recommendations. Even the most sophisticated clients are looking for advice—but only from sources they trust. For example, in 2012 investment bank advisory fees were up 15 percent despite merger deals nearly being at an all-time low. But a leading investment bank's advisory fees fell 26 percent over the same period of time because of an erosion of client trust caused by day-after-day reporting alleging violations.

Actions and words build or erode trust. Clients look beyond value, quality, and data. Clients recognize sales professionals they can trust when they are with them. As you prepare to have conversations with your clients, pay attention to what is happening emotionally. Ask yourself: What have you done for the client that you have not been paid for? What can you do? What do you know about the person you are selling to? What do you like about him or her? For clients you don't like (and it happens) find just one thing and keep your focus on that. Make the extra effort, and take the extra step.

> "It is a mistake to take subjective interactions out of the decision because subjectivity is the whole part."
> —David Brooks, New York Times columnist, PBS commentator

Summary

Aberdeen Group research continues to reinforce how important it is to create client *intimacy*. The business interpretation of this is to have deep knowledge about your clients and their industries. But intimacy has another meaning: closeness and friendship. A huge part of buying for almost all buyers is the experience. Working with tens of thousands of clients—and thousands in this new sales landscape—has proven to me that when clients feel you are there for them, they will go out of their way to be there for you. The president of a large technology company called me to say his team was evenly divided between the incumbent, a company whose system half of the dozen divisions reporting to him were already using, and us. The president was the tie breaker. His question to me was simple, "Can I trust you won't let me down?"

He was talking from his heart. It took trust to ask that question, and it took not only competency but also heart to respond. As you provide insights, ideas, and technical expertise to be client-focused, remember to be human-focused too.

> *"Informal conversations, that's how relationships are built."*
> —*Sheryl Sandberg, COO, Facebook*

Opening into the Future

Futuring, heat-mapping, value-tracking, phasing, and linking are labels I use to underscore change. The change in the social system between buyers and sellers is irreversible. The Internet has upended many of the old sales models. Much of what worked in the past is not working now. But who wants to go back? The best part about change is that it inspires progress. Change means risk, but it goes hand in hand with growth.

The trends explored in this book are more than labels—they represent a new way for you to relate to clients—as a thought partner. Through futuring you see around corners to anticipate and understand needs. Heat-mapping helps clients do the same, and value-tracking, phasing, and linking enable you to go around those corners together. Insights, ideas, consensus, business outcomes, proof of value, social media, sales tools, and client buying processes are the new conversation.

The speed of change is unprecedented, but one constant remains: relationships are built on trust. The values you bring to your clients still matter as much as the value you bring. While selling has changed and will never stop changing, the need for relationships has not changed.

You have chosen to be a salesperson, and with that choice comes the gift of resiliency. Every day you are called on to learn, listen, innovate, teach, and close. Your tools are new—and better. Your resources are unprecedented. You can be more insightful. Your product knowledge, industry knowledge, and client knowledge must go deeper than any time in sales. Selling today starts with how the client chooses to buy. This requires a kind of reverse engineering on your part—working backwards from business challenges into solutions. Research is essential, but so is keeping your eyes and ears open—and your heart.

The ideas in this book set the platform for success through new and relevant concepts, models, and skills. They build on consultative selling. Your success depends on your willingness and ability to help smart and connected clients become smarter and grow their businesses.

You have your own voice. Your talents are unique to you. You are surrounded by the forces of change. You must stretch and help your clients stretch. It is your job to anticipate the changes your clients are going through and respond quickly. By embracing change you will succeed and have more fun. The true challenge today is not in challenging clients. It is challenging yourself to raise the bar and forge a greater connection with your clients. You must be more curious, more persistent, and more motivated. Learn every day. Immerse yourself in your clients' businesses and solve their business problems. Become their thought partner. You will close more deals, and your clients will love and reward you for it.

Appendix

Sales Tools

Sales Ready Planner

Relationship: _____   Client Contact and Role: _____

Salesperson: _____   Team: _____

Date/Time: _____   Place/Phone: _____

Face-to-Face ☐   Phone ☐   Online ☐

Strategic Preparation

Where is your client in the buying cycle?

Stage 1: ☐	Stage 2: ☐	Stage 3: ☐	Stage 4, 5, 6: ☐
Awareness	Options	Research and Compare Solutions	Select, Negotiate, and Contract Execute Measure Business Outcome
(Pre–stage 1: Create Awareness)			

Where are you in the sales process?

Stage 1: ☐	Stage 2: ☐	Stage 3: ☐	Stage 4: ☐	Stage 5: ☐	Stage 6: ☐
Target and Qualify	Explore and Assess	Access and Develop	Position Solution, Refine, and Follow Up	Negotiate and Close	Deliver, Maintain, and Expand

Client: Decision maker ☐   Influencer ☐   User ☐   Coach ☐   Third party ☐

Measurable call objective: _____

_____

_____

(continued)

Call Strategy

Agenda	Accountability	Role	Time

Client Preparation

Summary/main issue from last contact:		Opening/rapport/leveraging readiness:		
Customer's business challenge/needs:		Industry issues:		
Decision-making process: executive/stakeholders:		Time frame:	Compelling event:	Current costs/budget:

Insights/Ideas

Insights and knowledge sharing:		Application to client:	
Reserve/data:			
Questions to ask:		Idea/Solution:	
Success story/examples:	Competitive strategy:		Financial impact:
Materials for meeting:			

Debrief

Objective achieved: Yes □ No □	Next steps:
New information:	Time:
Opportunity:	Clients:

Value Map

Name: _____   Client: _____

Key Business Challenge Client Objectives			
Stakeholders/Roles	Stakeholder 1	Stakeholder 2	Stakeholder 3
Business Challenge			
Business Outcome			
Proof of Success (success story, examples, referrals)			
Proof of Value/ ROI/Reduce Risk			
Personal Drivers			
Other Priorities			
Your Customized Solution Connected to Business Outcome			

Insight Statement Template

An Insight Statement is a "LEAD-IN" to a business challenge dialogue and leads to your strength. It is not a time to make your pitch. Present your insight in an objective manner.

Company: _____ Contact/Role: _____ Client/Prospect _____

Business Challenge (researched/assumed): _____

Position the Business Challenge (Leverage your experience and knowledge to focus the conversation on a business issue you believe your prospect is concerned about and that leads to your strengths)

┌───┐
│   │
│   │
│   │
└───┘

Support Insight with Data (Use research, hard metrics, experience, expertise to ideally teach your client something he/she does not know or to broaden his/her perspective and cause the client to challenge the status quo):

┌───┐
│   │
│   │
│   │
└───┘

Support with a Success Story (Keep story brief/relevant and show ROI)

┌───┐
│   │
│   │
│   │
└───┘

Ask for Client/Prospect's Experience or Perspective (Learn how your prospect feels about the insight; don't ask for commitment)

┌───┐
│   │
│   │
│   │
└───┘

Resolving Objections

Relate/Acknowledge/ Empathize	Yes	No	Feedback/ Examples
■ Acknowledge/empathize	☐	☐	
■ Reinforce you are listening	☐	☐	
■ Connect with client	☐	☐	
■ Pave the way for your question	☐	☐	
Question			Feedback/ Examples
■ Narrow down broad objections/identify the underlying concern	☐	☐	
■ Continue to use acknowledgment and drill down	☐	☐	
Position			Feedback/ Examples
■ Tailor your response to client's specific concern	☐	☐	
■ Support with data, as possible	☐	☐	
■ Tie to business outcome	☐	☐	
■ Support with example	☐	☐	
Check			Feedback/ Examples
■ Ask for feedback	☐	☐	
■ Probe and position as needed	☐	☐	

Win–Loss

Salesperson: _____   **Third-party debrief conducted:** _____

Client interviewed: _____   **By:** _____ **Date:** _____

Competitors: _____   **Opportunity:** _____

                                        Won by: _____

LOSS REVIEW

Solution Fit with Client Need	
1. What was the reason for our losing the business? 2. What were the top two deciding factors in your decision? 3. How did our solution align with your business challenge and meet your needs? 4. How did we compare in: 　■ Pricing 　■ Technical solution 　■ Value beyond the product solution 　■ Ease of working with us 　■ Senior presence	5. How would you describe the quality of our proposal in meeting your needs? 6. Where did we rank in the final list of competitors? Why? 7. What was the key strengths of the winning provider? 8. How would you describe the effectiveness of X [salesperson]? To help [him/her] grow professionally, what was your organization's perception of [his/her] strengths/areas for development? Sales team? Support team? Executive presence?
Win Review	
What are the top two reasons we won? What did our solution offer technically? What did we bring outside the technical solution that added value and differentiated us? How innovative was our solution? How did our pricing compare? How effective was our team?	What would you have liked to see in our solution? What were our points of differentiation? What were our strengths? Was there a close contender? If so, who? What tipped the scales in our favor?
Future Opportunities	
(If we won the opportunity:) What do we need to keep doing or working on to create the most positive experience?	(If we lost the opportunity:) Would you consider us for future needs? What advice would you give us to help us better meet your needs and work with you in the future?

Index

About the Author

Linda Richardson is the founder of Richardson, a global sales performance company where she serves as executive chairwoman. She teaches sales and management courses at the Wharton Graduate School of the University of Pennsylvania and the Wharton Executive Development Center. Her most recent book, *Perfect Selling*, was a *New York Times* bestseller and received the SBA gold medal for best sales book. Richardson is credited with starting the consultative sales movement, which has guided most sales methodologies used by companies for the past few decades.